A Joy to See

Ekphrastic Poetry
based on the artwork of

Kay Levine

Orchestrated by Sherri Levine

Cover Painting by Kay Levine
Design & Layout
Dale Champlin

Published by
Just a Lark Books
308 SE Walnut Street

JUST A LARK BOOKS
Hillsboro, Oregon

Body copy set in Minion Pro

First edition

10 9 8 7 6 5 4 3 2 1

ISBN 9798889557180

A thing of beauty is a joy forever:
its loveliness increases;
it will never pass into nothingness.

—John Keats

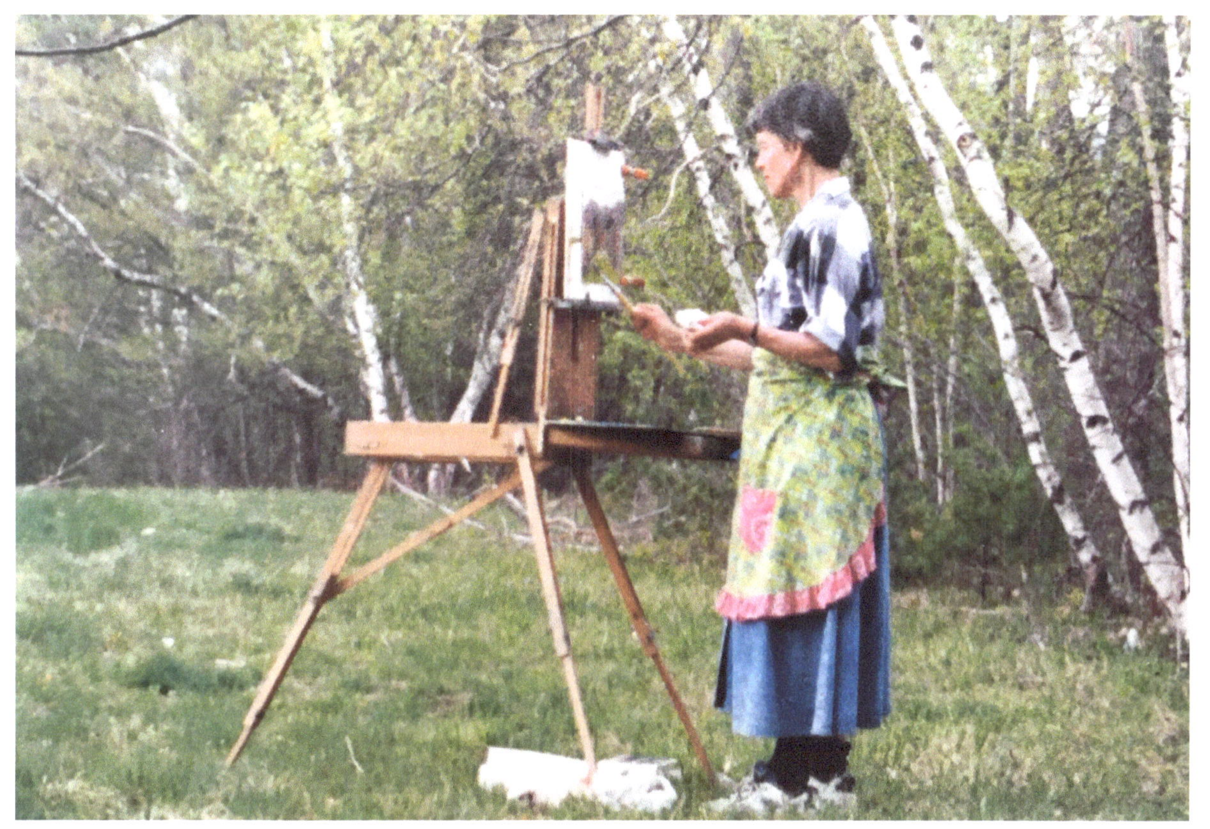

Kay Levine en Plein Air

A Joy to See

Ekphrastic Poetry
based on the artwork of

Kay Levine

Orchestrated by Sherri Levine

TABLE OF CONTENTS

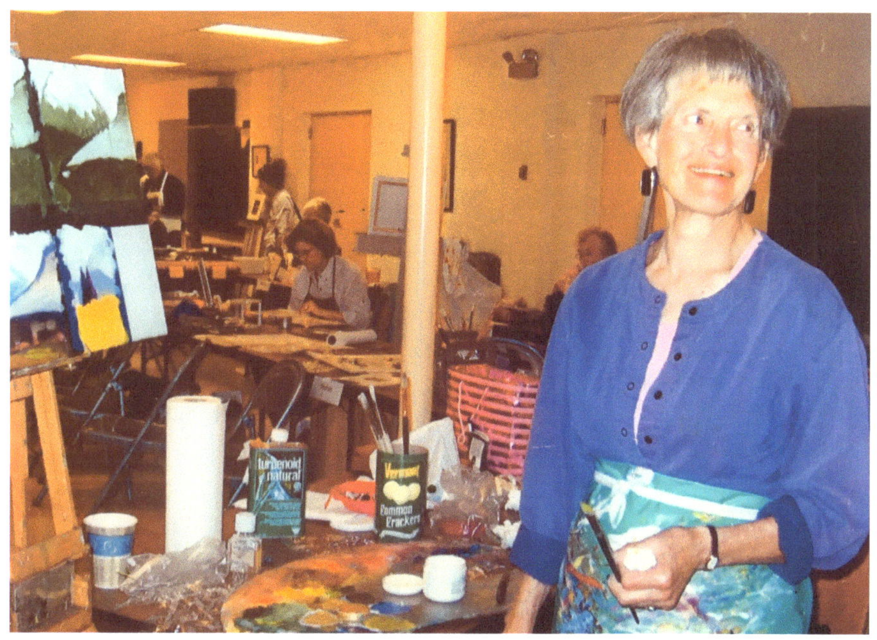

My mother, Kay Levine, born Kay Weissman, was my best friend. She was an incredible artist, mother, and grandmother. Born in 1937 in the Washington Heights neighborhood of New York City, she started painting at a young age. She earned her Bachelor's degree at Michigan State University and her Master's Degree from Yeshiva University, Stanford University, and St. Rose College in Albany, New York where she lived until she moved to Portland, Oregon to be close to her family.

She studied art at the Arts Students League and Woodstock School of Art. Her mentor, Zhang Huan, said she "was a master colorist." Her medium was mostly oil, though some of these paintings included in this book are pastel and watercolor.

She was also an educator. She taught art to children and literacy to adults, seniors, and to prisoners in maximum-security prisons such as Sing Sing. I was in awe of her; she was rarely afraid and usually determined to do what she wanted to do.

My mother understood my passion for poetry. She came to most of my poetry readings and to the events that I hosted. She was a special friend whom I profoundly miss.

—Sherri Levine, Kay Levine's Daughter

Matthew Dickman
Paulann Petersen
Andrea Hollander
Lex Runciman
Susan Woods Morse
Ann Farley
Dale Champlin
Willa Schneberg
Fran Payne Adler
Leanne Grabel
Nitza M. Hernández López
Marilyn Johnston
Shawn Aveningo-Sanders
Emmett Wheatfall
Nancy Christopherson
John Sibley Williams
Lois Rosen
Sebastian Arias
Paola Vergara
Jennifer Dorner
Peter M. Gordon
Norma Edythe Heyser
Patti Palmer-Baker
Marc Janssen
Francis Opila
John C. Morrison
Penelope Scambly Schott
Sherri Levine

THIS MORNING

I sat watching my kids throw

each other around

the living room, laughing,

alive in the small muscles

they have been growing

like flowers. Pink and orange

beneath their skin. They are not

gardens, they are human.

Parents like to say

to their kids: I gave you life.

That's true. But what we don't

say is that we have

also given them death. Given

them both spring and winter.

The morning and the mourning.

—Matthew Dickman

    —after Kay Levine, *Shocking Pink*

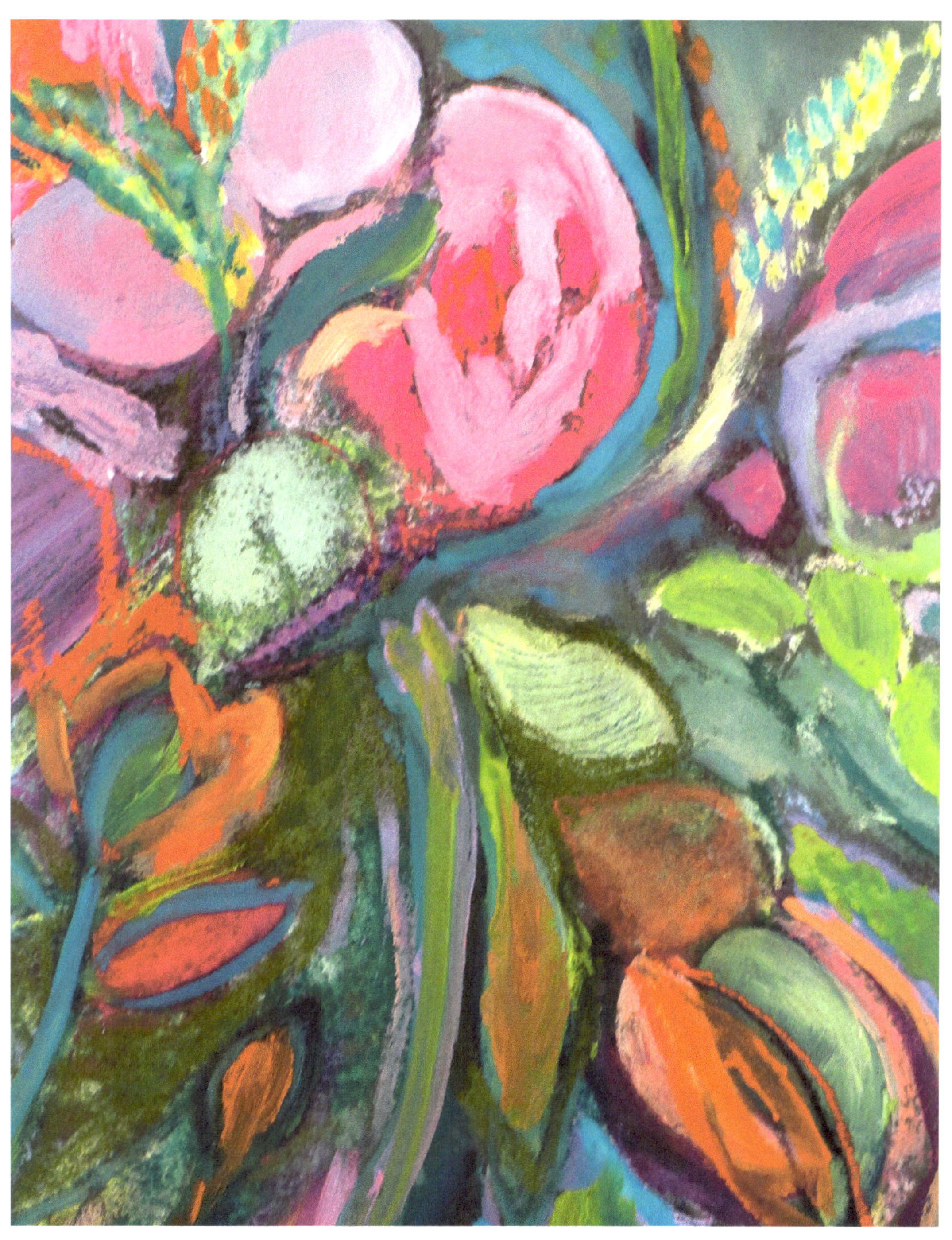

Shocking Pink by Kay Levine

MOTHER TREE, DAUGHTER TREE

—after Kay Levine, *Beautiful Blossoms*

See how each one pours

her warmth

into the other.

When these two

unfurl themselves

into a froth of blossom,

even that deepness

named winter

gives way.

—Paulann Petersen

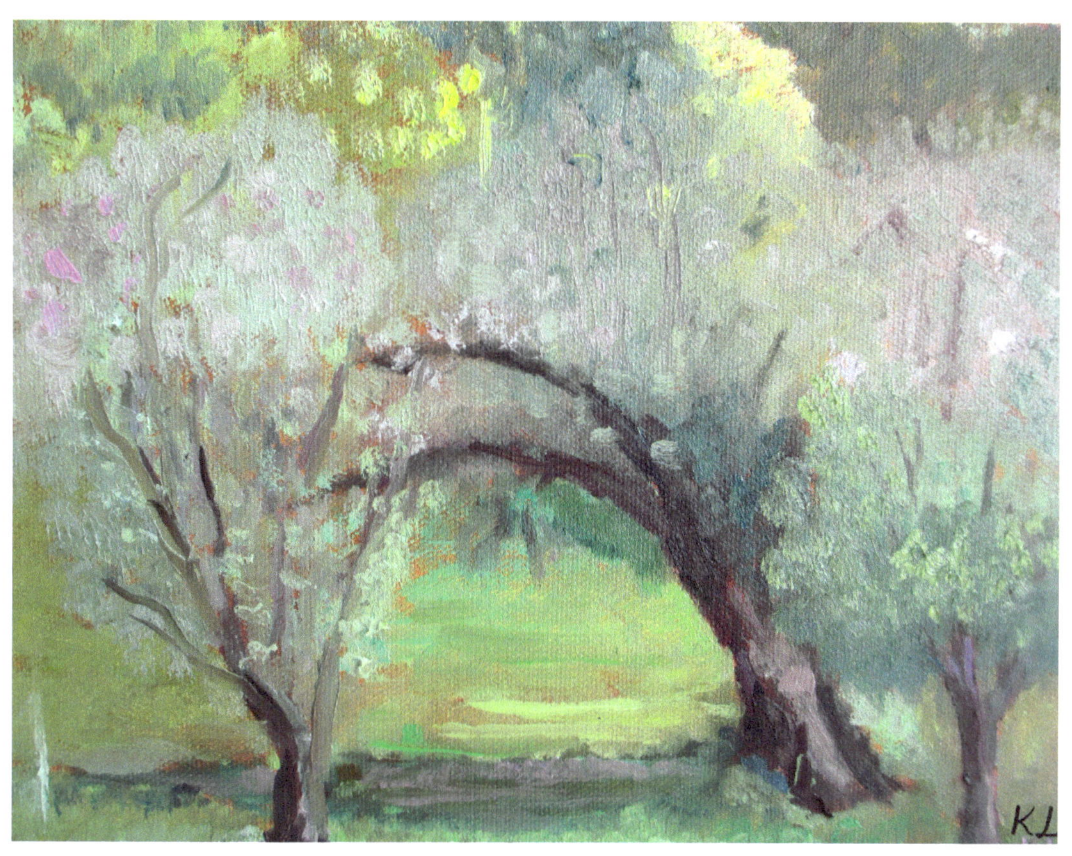

Beautiful Blossoms by Kay Levine

THREE PINK ROSES

—after Kay Levine, *Rose Trio*

Out in the garden,

they were simply roses

among roses. But here

in the house, they linger

together in a glass pitcher

placed in the exact center

of a small, round, nonchalant

table accustomed to minding

only its own drab business

in the far corner of the room.

Wide enough to hide the old

pitcher's chipped spout,

their blooms transform

the dull yellow wall

to blazing gold.

—Andrea Hollander

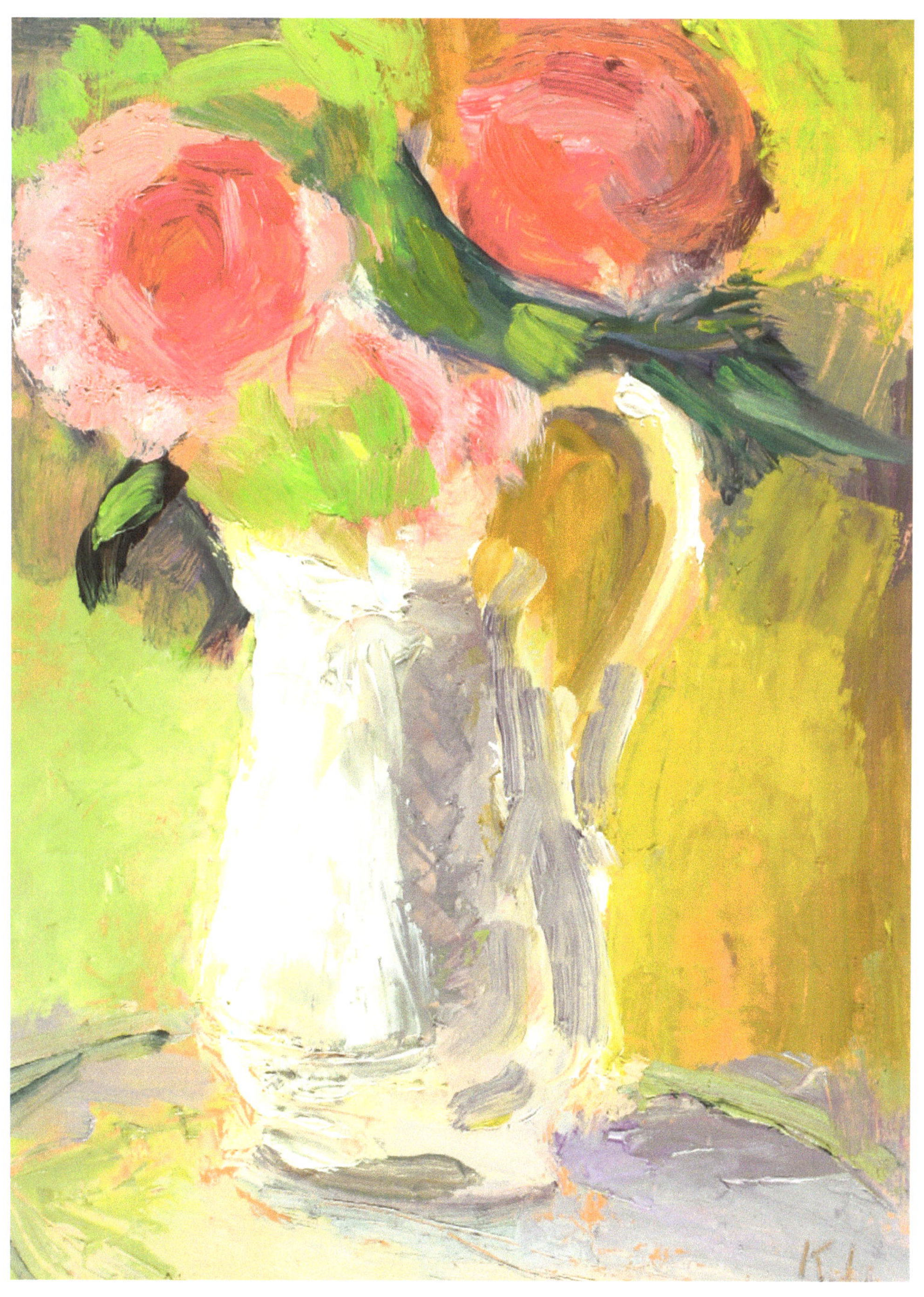

Rose Trio by Kay Levine

—after Kay Levine, *Saratoga Park*

Black fire smoke in its roiling, acrid hurry.
Home dug graves where once the washing hung.
A child's face, silent eyes that merely look at you,
blink, eyes beyond crying. Snow falling says cold,
does not say beautiful. And yet that child
will remember summer's trees lush with color,
sturdy trees to climb in, trunks brown gray
and the canopies all green and crosshatching,
small wind, blur and yellow under sky mostly blue.
And one day the child grown will find a place
to rest on a grassy meadow bed—to lean back,
head in laced hands, and breathe deep, close eyes,
doze, wake, look up, look up and wonder.

—Lex Runciman

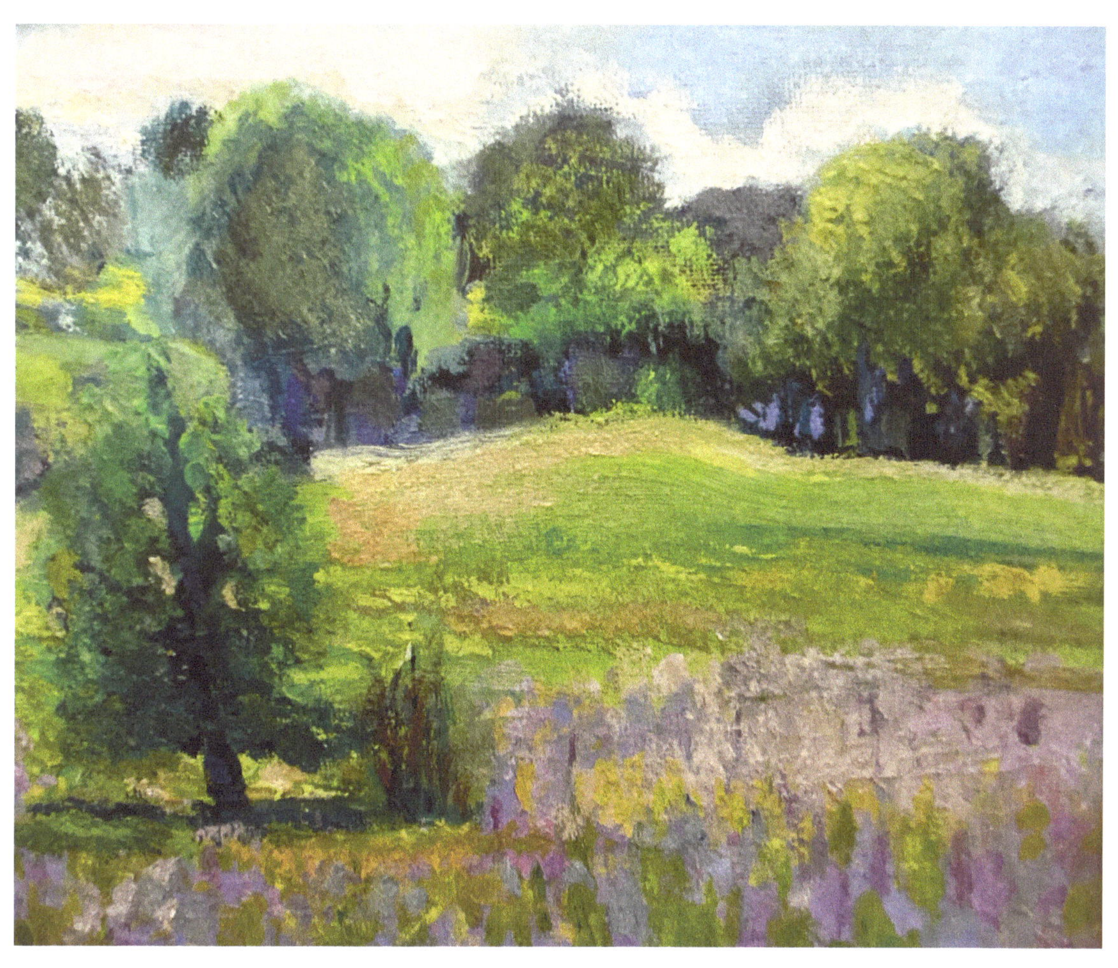

Saratoga Park by Kay Levine

—after Kay Levine, *Irises*

Purple iris thrive here, crowned
wing tips fluttering in the breeze.

As your paintings came alive,
I cherished a child's wonder of memories,

your face my inner sanctum,
everywhere breaths of beauty.

Iris with cream-colored hearts
hidden deep, like your smile,

recalling a delicate rustle of personalities
wafted from you to me and back again,
paintings and flowers resolute,
blossoming tall in my imaginings
with the ephemeral fragrance of purple —

our lives, their fragility, held for too short a time,
all the more precious in this stately elegance
with their refusal to bow down to incoming rains.

—Susan Woods Morse

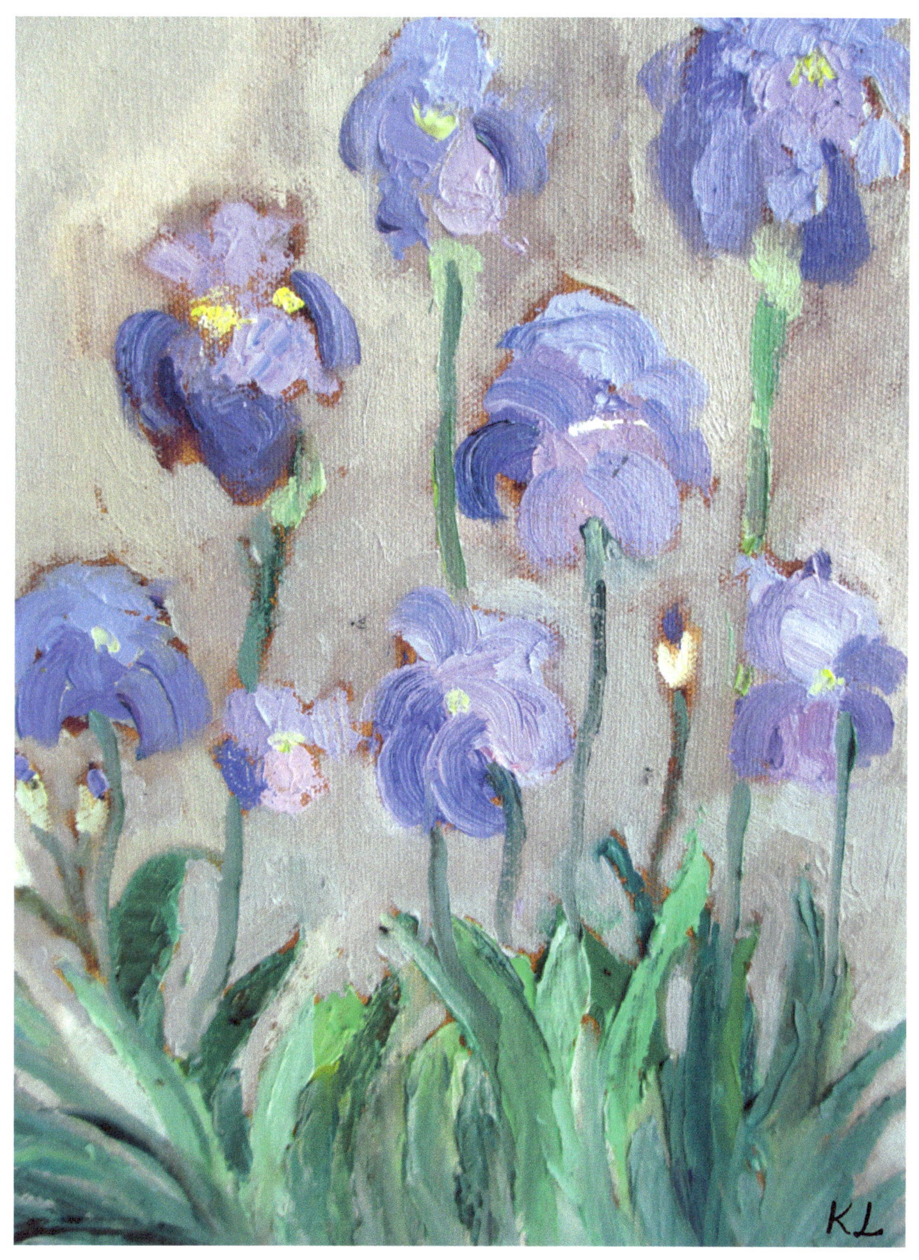

Irises by Kay Levine

in this painting, would you reach

and smooth blossoms with fingertips, rearrange?

Lean in, press cheek to petals, breathe

deeply of pink and green?

Would you shrink to curl in curve,

tuck in shadow, slip stem, sleep on a leaf ?

Or smaller yet, would you be pigment afloat

in oily sheen—cobalt blue, vermilion, ochre,

indigo, red madder, lead white—mixed

and layered to suggest line, shape, shadow?

Would you be a swirl of lavender,

illusion of white light on glossy vase?

Is this how you shine?

—Ann Farley

    —after Kay Levine, *Masterpiece*

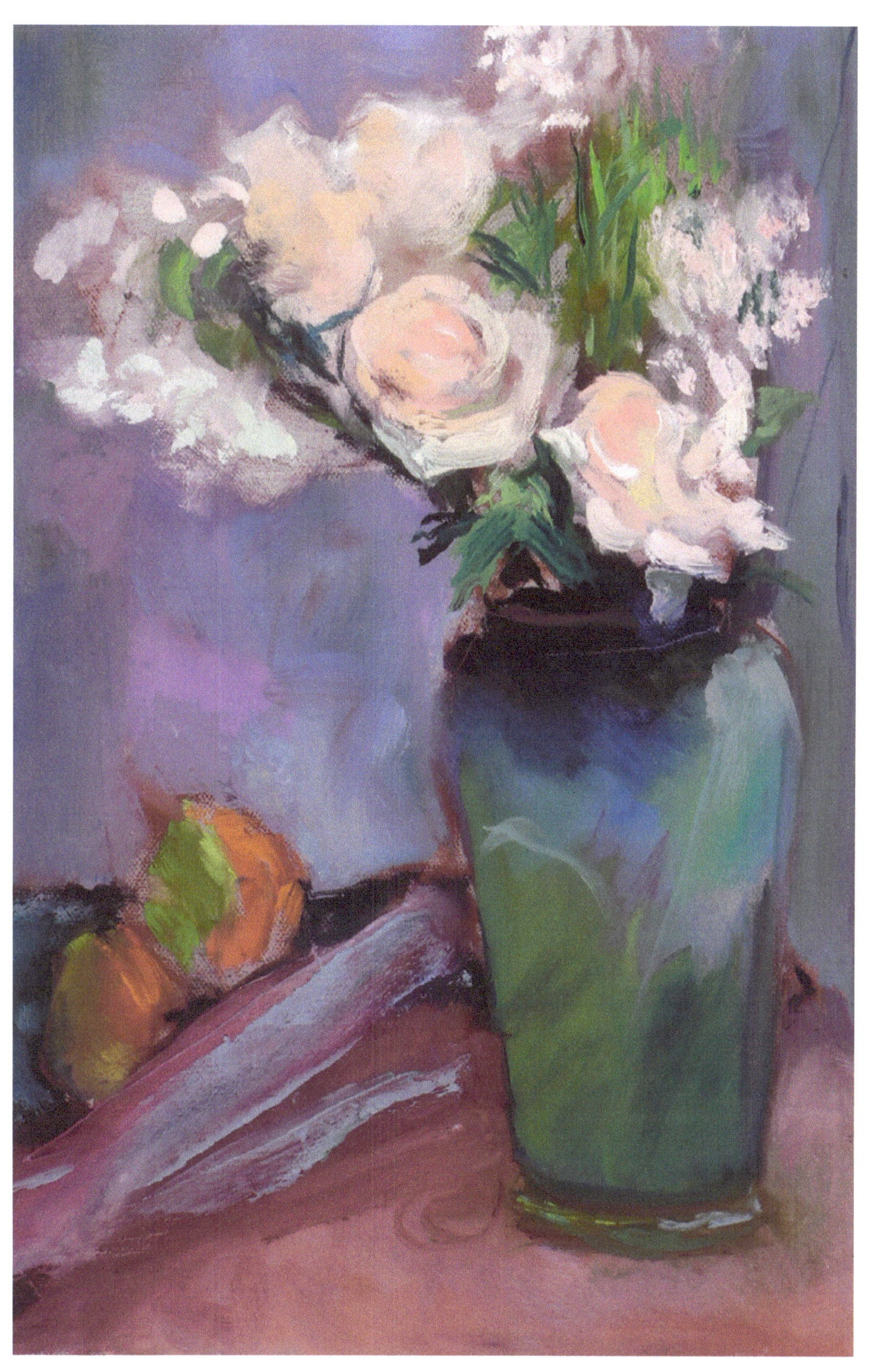

Masterpiece by Kay Levine

FIRST BLUSH

  —after Kay Levine, *Red Rose*

The room is quiet—
ocean-green and lilac
  not noisy red.

I want to be rosy red—
the tall blushing blossom,
not the bloom
  beginning to
    droop.

I wish to beguile a man,
entice him to pluck me
  from blue-green water,

trim my long stem,
strip me of my leaves,
snip off my thorns,
and thread me
  into his lapel.

—Dale Champlin

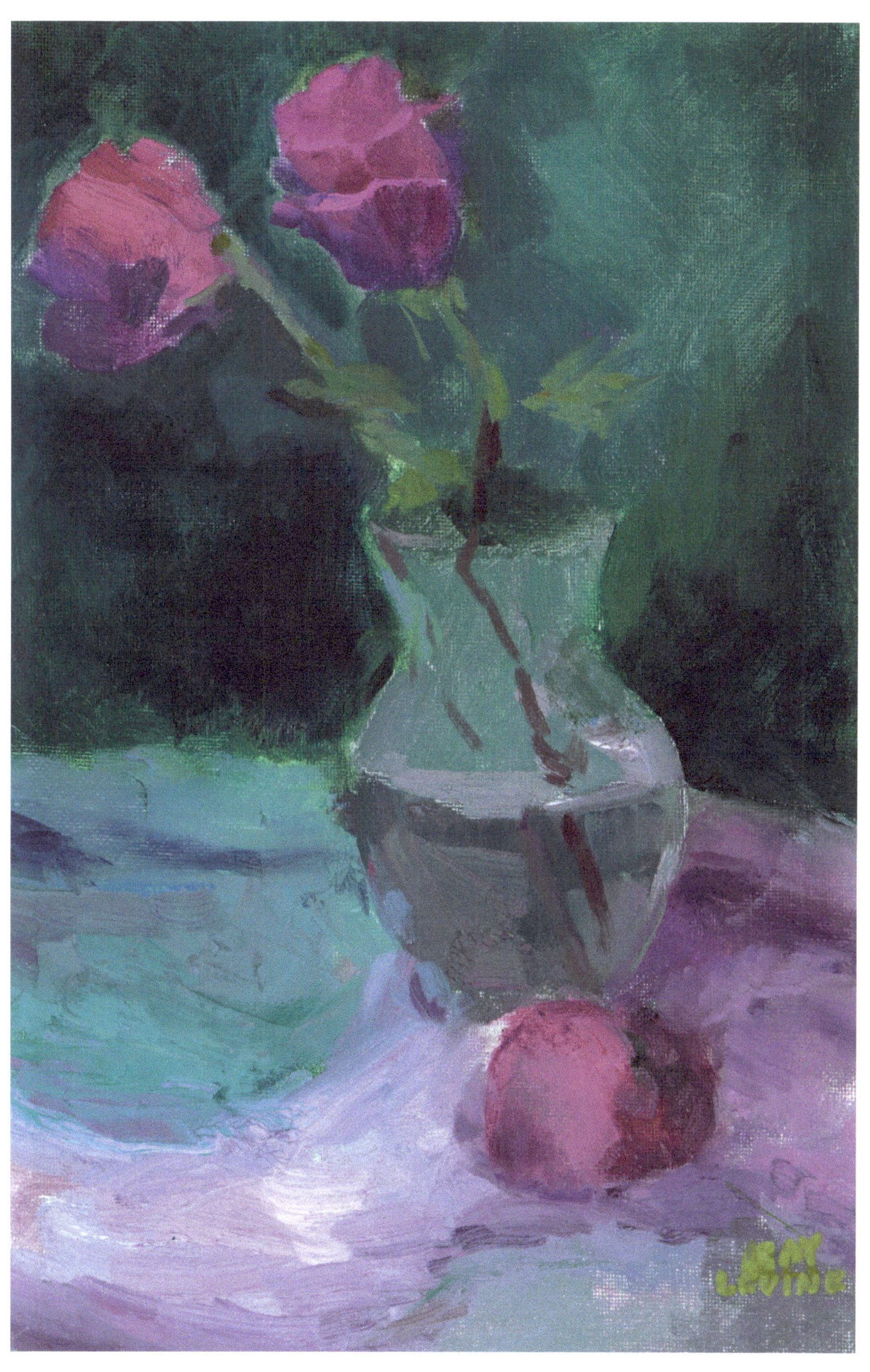

Red Rose by Kay Levine

LAMENT

> —after Kay Levine, *Shana Tova*

The shofar holds my agony
and the world's. When I blow
it can't help itself, it quavers my grief
and yours. From the mountain it intones.
The moon and stars catch our anguish,
echo it back with thousands
of simultaneous thunders.
We want what we want
and lament what we cannot get.
We don't want to suffer or die.
I hold the ram's curly horn to my lips.
Where is the ram?
Is he wearing his other horn?

—Willa Schneberg

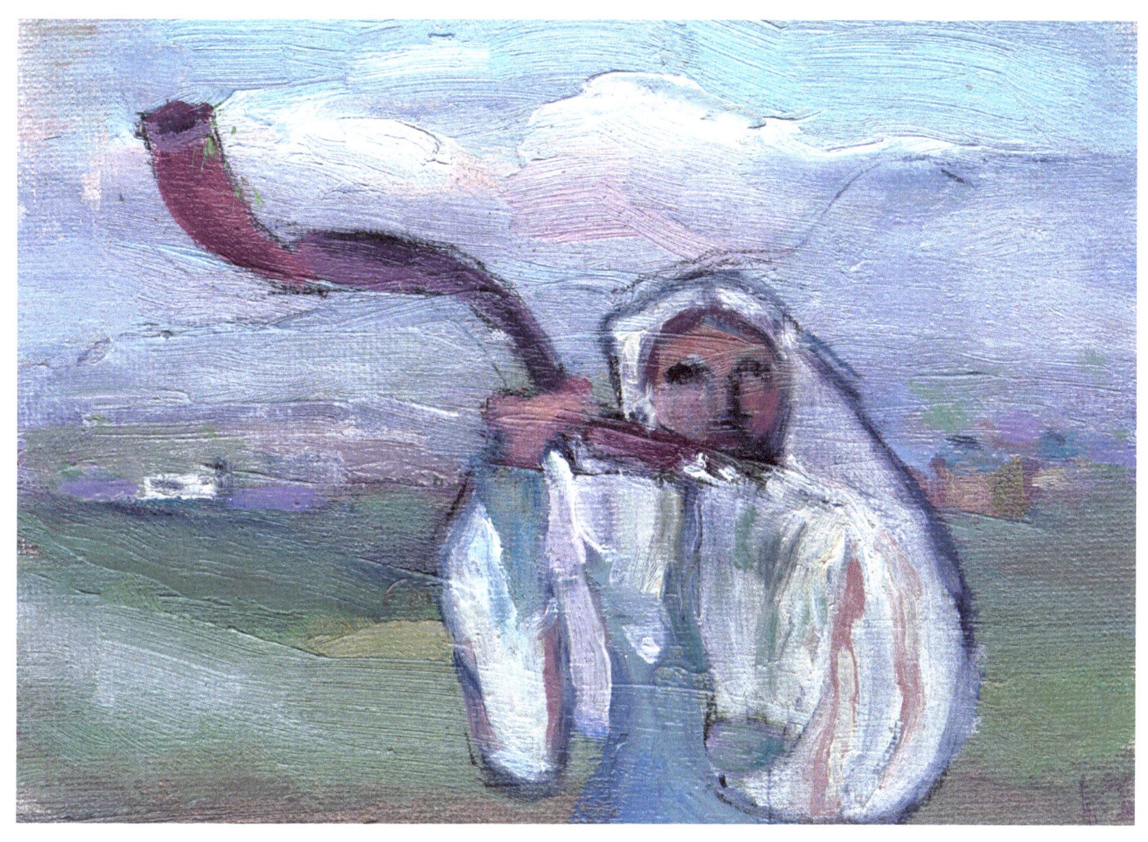

Shana Tova by Kay Levine

SINGING IN DARK TIMES

> —after Kay Levine, *Red Scarf*

> *In the dark times*
> *Will there also be singing?*
> *Yes, there will also be singing.*
> *About the dark times.*
>
> —Bertolt Brecht

She'd resisted fear all her life,

now, this, stirred from sleep in her bed, she

ran, choking, photo faces of her family in smoke,

shoes, passports, the doorframe's *mezuzah* melted

What she needed, she told us, days after hate

scrawled *Die, Juden,* on synagogue walls,

scorched the Muslim Center, was hurled

at her home, blazing the halls

Song, she said, *I need song*

and ceremony, my sisters around me

We will hold her in song, weave the silk

of guitar song around her, surround her with love

—Frances Payne Adler

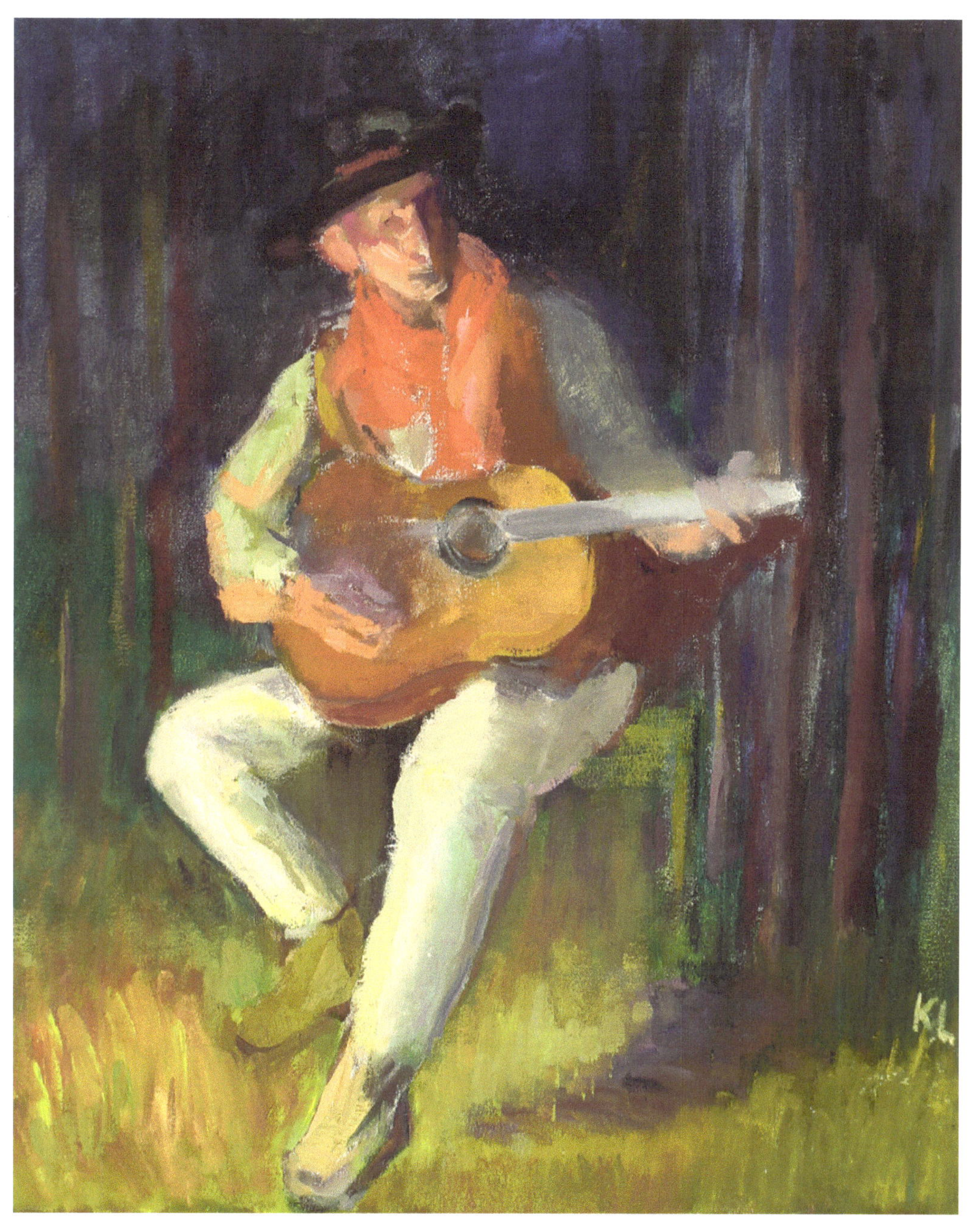

Red Scarf by Kay Levine

THE MEADOW & THE REVOLUTION

    —after Kay Levine, *Cone Flower*

Camus said a day would come when

revolutions would have need of beauty.

Is it today? Will it be enough?

I could gather this soft meadow

these coneflowers and their spectral friends

into my boxes, like tefillin.

And I could wrap the straps around my biceps

around my forehead and

feel the large power of soft beauty.

Beyond the smooth of the pinks

beyond the small globes of fertility

These flowers could heal us. We could eat them.

And then a burst of lobelia

would shame our spilled blood.

—Leanne Grabel

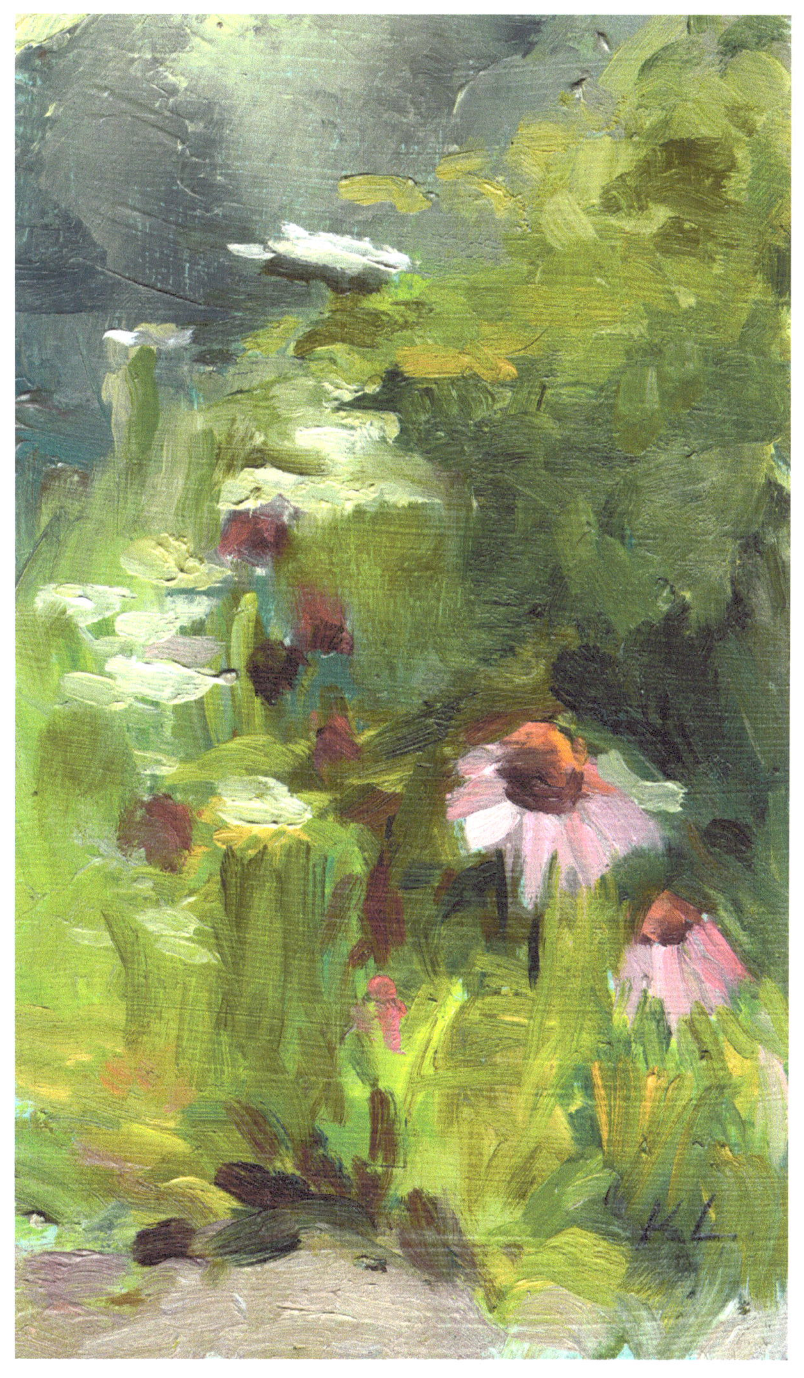

Cone Flower by Kay Levine

MIGHTY PRESENCE

—after Kay Levine, *Chartreuse*

It appeared standing proudly
on a lime green foliage ground,
that imposing flower vase
holding a lush bouquet of roses
dark green leaves and upright stems.

It emerged from the ground up
full of pinkish laughing roses
on a heavy sunset day
with a dark maroon sky wall
like an omen on display.

With only one curved handle
and a body of pink reflection
that vase has a mighty presence
something leveled and mysterious.

A suggestive flower vase
so determined to stay grounded.

—Nitza M. Hernández López

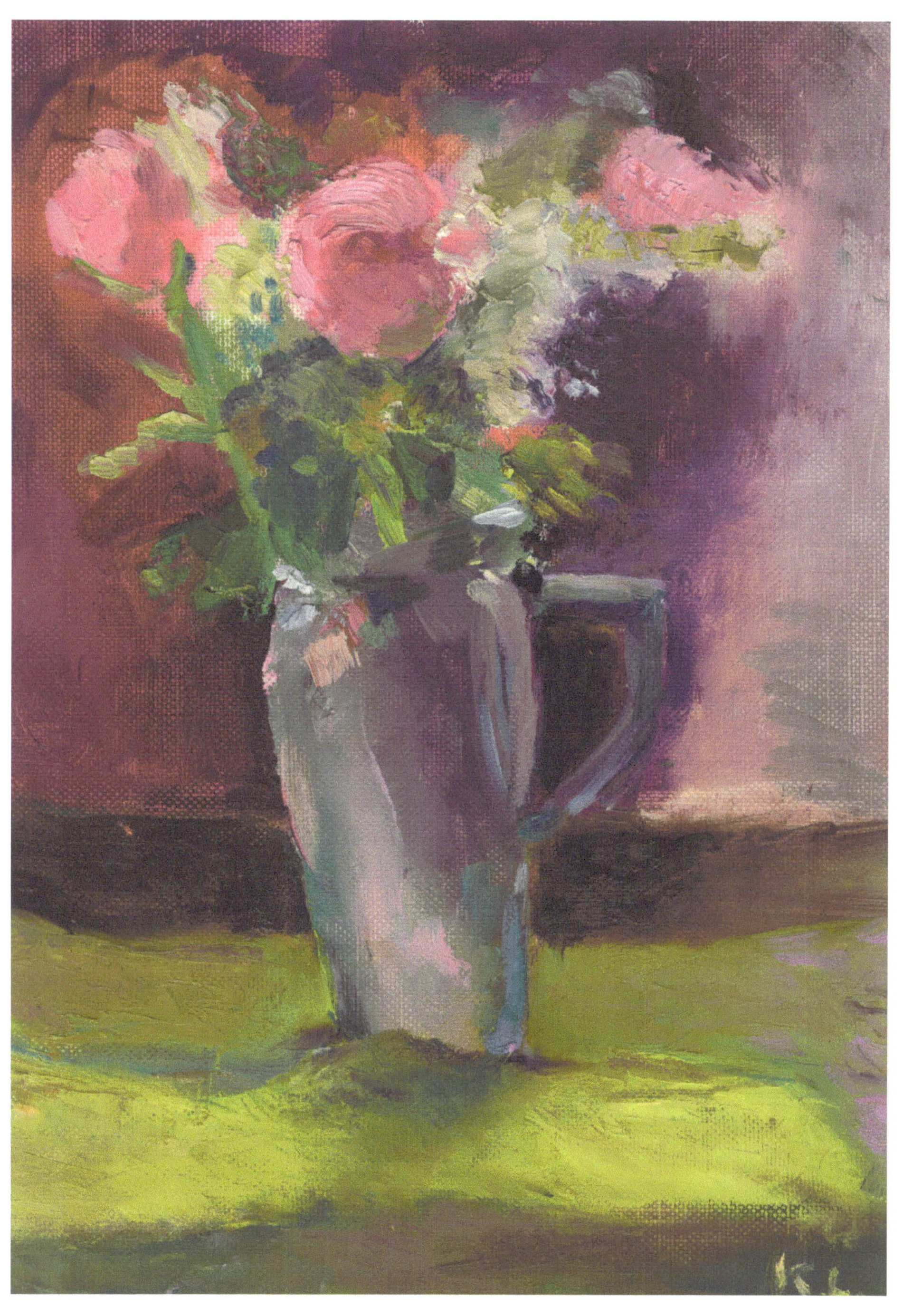

Chartreuse by Kay Levine

WHEN MY DAUGHTER ASKS HOW SHE'LL KNOW
SHE'S IN LOVE

—after Kay Levine, *View from Vashon Island*

I tell her to recall that first time, at sunrise,

as she carried her kayak to the water's edge,

her back to the island, how she followed

the call of a heron and an osprey as it

returned to the nest to feed its young.

How it felt to float with the current—

sometimes slow and steady, sometimes

the thrill of rapids, on the way downstream.

Or, maybe, that moment, on the drive home,

as the sunset painted its crimson palette

on the mountainside. How, with each, she

says, it was as if the ground shook beneath her.

I tell her falling in love can be like all of this.

To wait, let it unfold in front of her, unhurried.

—Marilyn Johnston

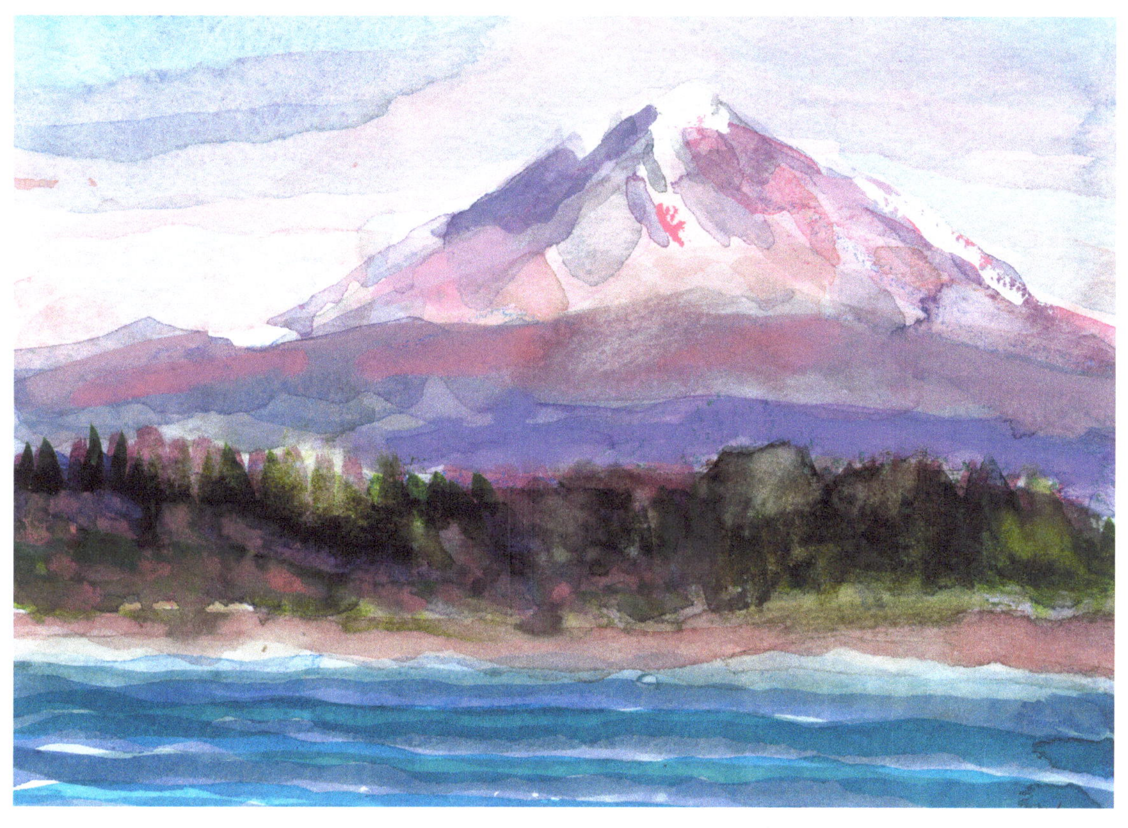

View from Vashon Island by Kay Levine

—after Kay Levine, *Le Jardin*

What I remember most is her hospitality, how there was always
room for one more at her table. How that red roof was a beacon—
all are welcome here. How she loved to cook, to feed friends
and strangers alike. How each meal was a gathering, an invitation
to break bread and share a story. There was always sangria
and a vase bursting with fresh-plucked blooms.
Oh, how the late-day sun would bathe the room
as daydreams floated over hills painted green and pink
and lilac. Such a kaleidoscope of purples! How I loved
to walk and talk to pink dogwood trees—their bark
holding years of a young girl's secrets. For me, home
will always be an old house in the hills, a long, weathered
wood plank table in the kitchen, and priscilla-curtained
windows open to a garden surrounded by a field of lilac trees.

—Shawn Aveningo-Sanders

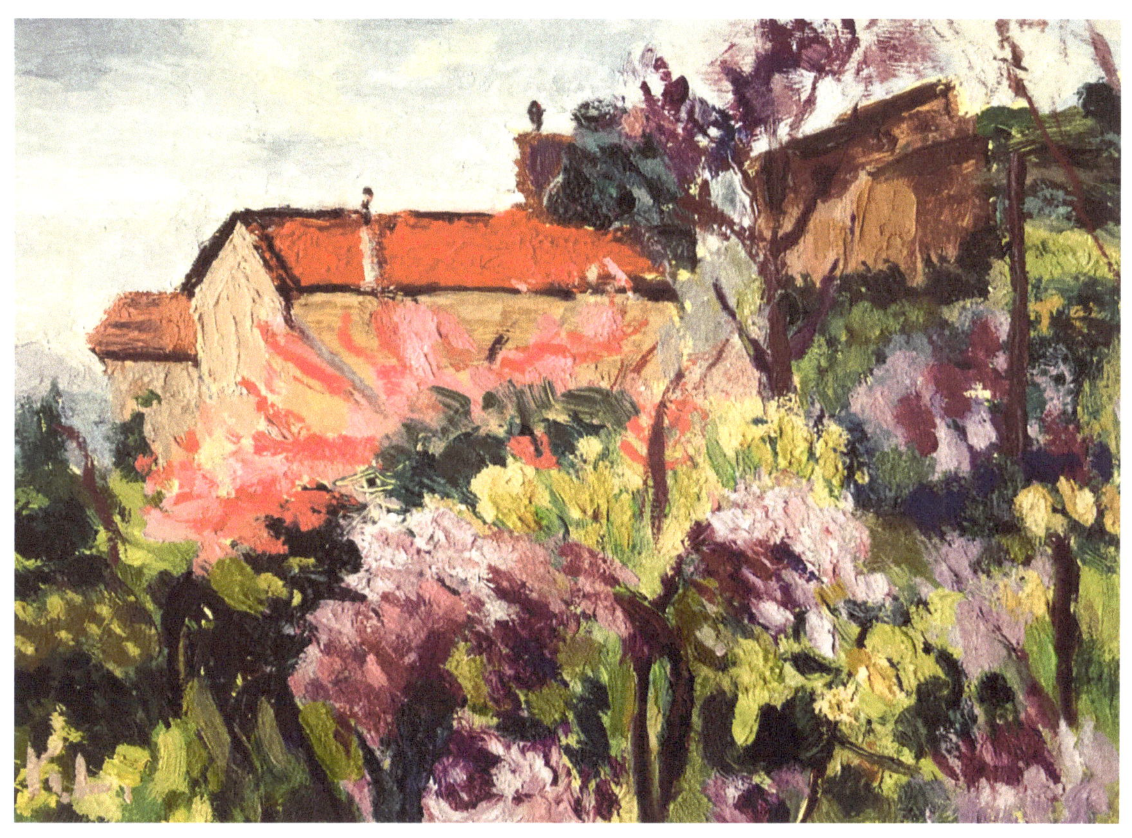

Le Jardin by Kay Levine

MY MOTHER'S INSPIRATION

—after Kay Levine, *Electric Blue*

My mother's inspiration.

A bouquet of blossoms.

Long stem pedicles.

Her petals spread like open palms.

A psalm implied? Not with

Flowery words, but feminine.

Gaze at them. They thirst.

Do you thirst? Once wet

Pastel colors have dried.

You do thirst. If you find

You need more or less

Of the feminine,

Her petals spread like open palms.

Gaze at them. Stare long.

Like open palms they care.

My mother's inspiration.

A bouquet of blossoms.

—Emmett Wheatfall

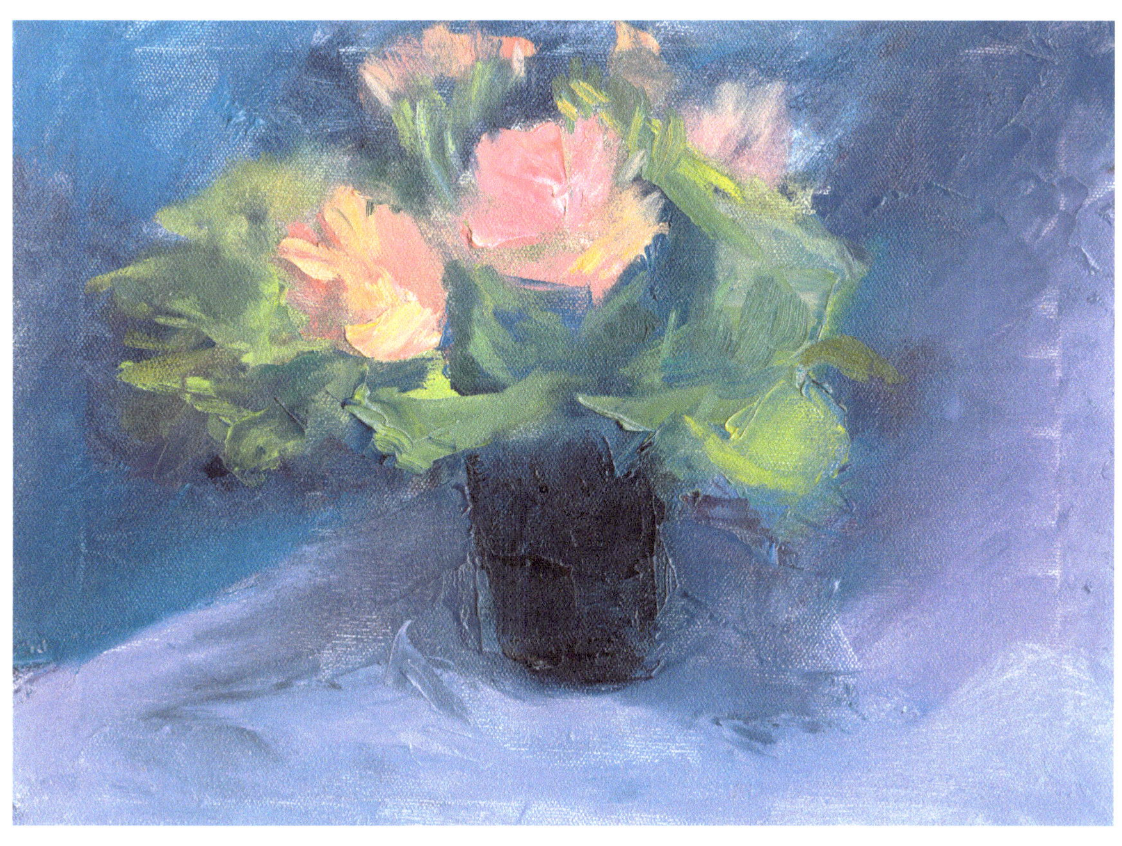

Electric Blue by Kay Levine

—after Kay Levine, *Woman Reading Poetry*

Notice the texture of the canvas not quite filled in.
Most prominent her dearest comportment, presented—
she, leaning lightly back in her kitchen chair after filling
the children's baskets with figs and bread and soft
cheese at water's edge.

Note the red camellia at the base of her hair lifted—
where someone, perhaps even she, has pinned it. Maybe
after making love along a tender spring path in late
afternoon. What she holds quietly between her fingertips
is one secret only she can disclose, if she chooses,
and calls you over.

—Nancy Christopherson

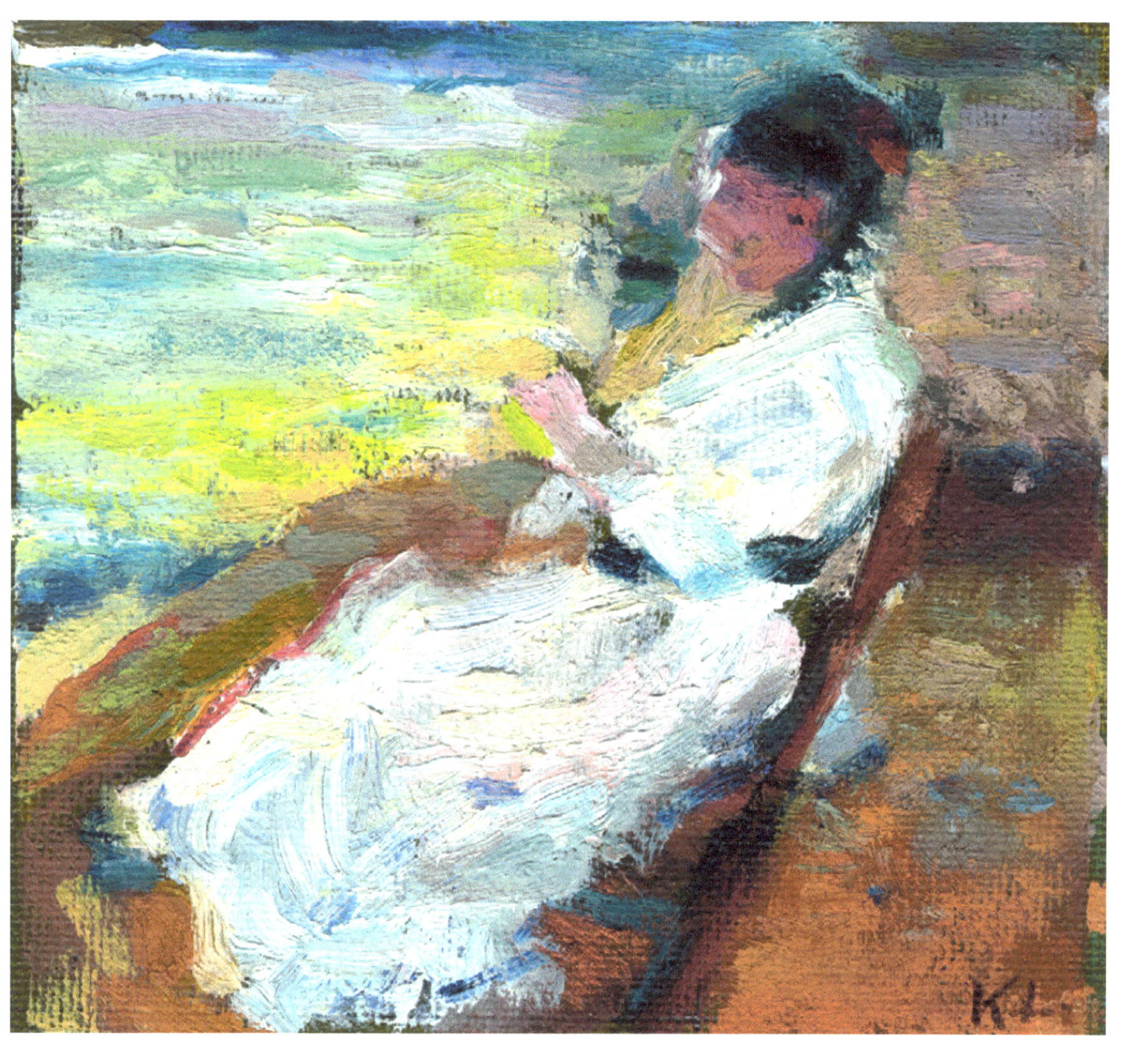

Woman Reading Poetry by Kay Levine

TORCH

—after Kay Levine, *Torch*

A cloud never dies
—Thich Nhat Hanh

Like a talisman, like a lost heaven still
breathing its stars, her wild yellow flame
reaches up through our shared dark toward these
never-dying clouds that just keep adopting
the faces of those we cannot stop loving.
It's been too long called sacrifice. Grief.
That there is hope within such a smudged
canvass, such a deeply textured absence,
suggests you are still here, Mom, in this shorn
light, this bruised bird's cry. With enough ash,
enough yes, I am convinced I can rebuild in me
your enduring fire, and all its necessary shadows.

—John Sibley Williams

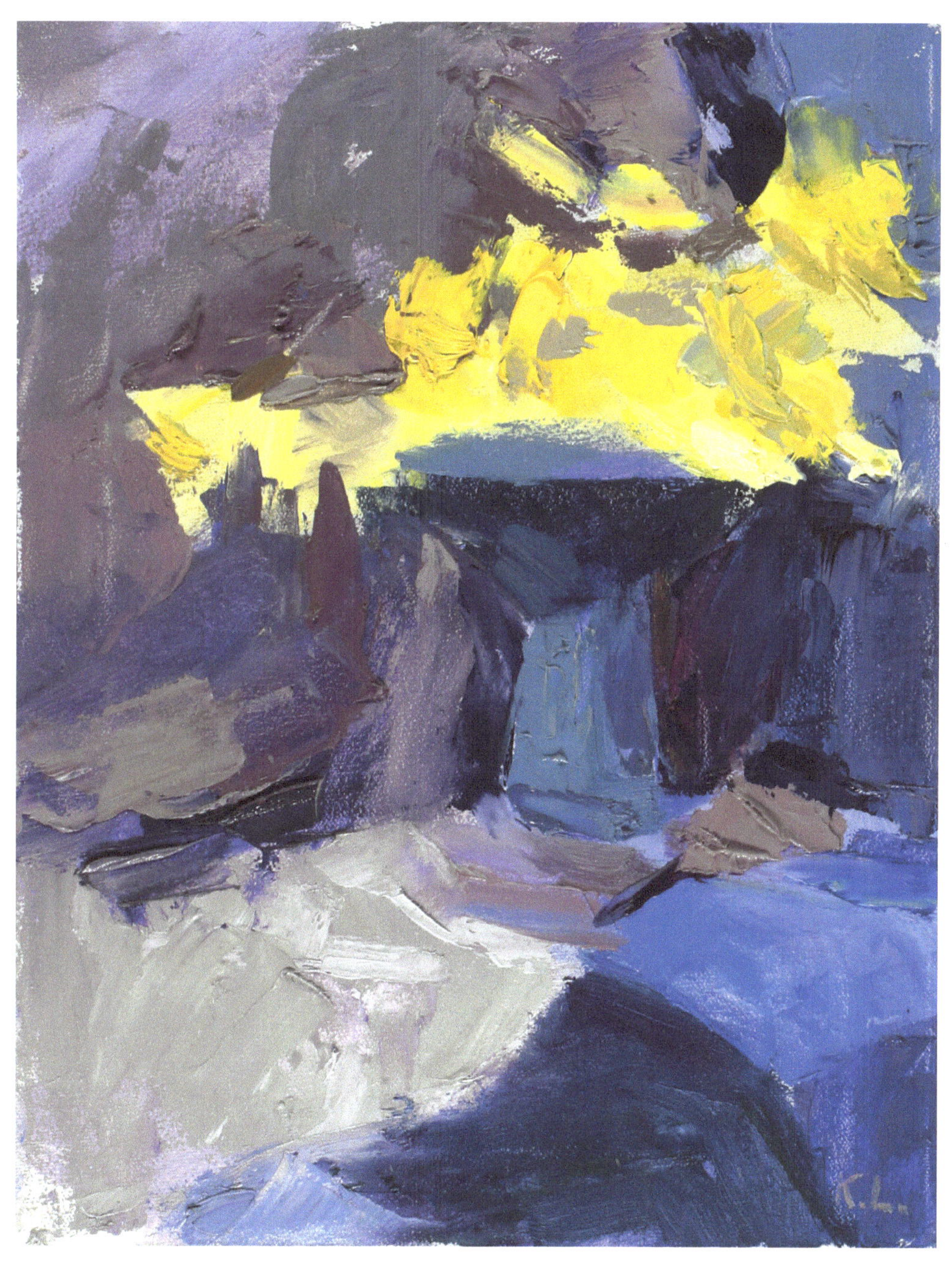

Torch by Kay Levine

KAY'S CACTUS

    —after Kay Levine, *Kay's Cactus*

The cactus yearns for wildness

Bracts curve like dancers' arms

Flinging jade and mint green shades

Daubed under rose-pink charms

The deeper ruby floral center

Thickens as layers spread wide

Horizontal sprays gather

Arcing as warm shades collide

This Thanksgiving cactus bursts

Spring color in tropical places

Where pastel flushes astonish with joy

Kay's art has no thorns, it embraces

—Lois Rosen

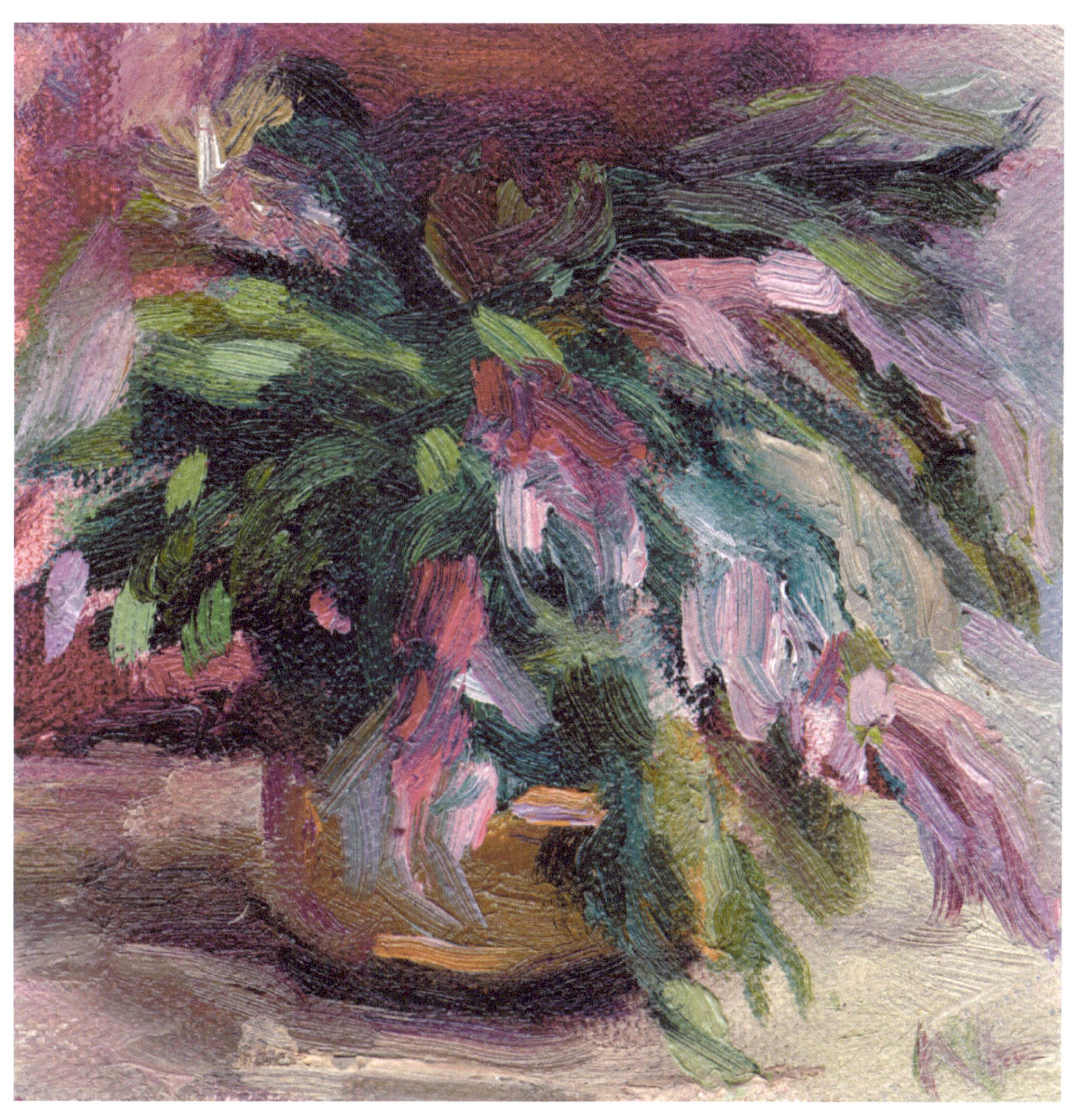

Kay's Cactus by Kay Levine

O T O Ñ O

>   —en honor a Kay Levine, *Autumn in New York*

Arden en llamas cobrizas
las cabelleras de esos gigantes,
mientras resisten el tiempo
un suelo vigoroso les sirve como base.
Silueta desgarrada sobre el cielo.
¿Acaso son montañas?
La calma es una cuerda tensa
en ese instante previo a la caída.
Óxido, ocre, musgo
estallan desde el centro.
Pigmentos de una edad dorada
paisaje de rompecabezas.

A U T U M N

>   —after Kay Levine, *Autumn in New York*

They burn in coppery flames
the hair of those giants,
as they resist time
a vigorous soil serves as its base.
Torn silhouette over the sky.
Are they mountains?
Calm is a tight rope
in that moment before the downfall.
Rust, ochre, moss
burst from the center.
Pigments from a golden age
puzzle landscape.

—Sebastian Arias

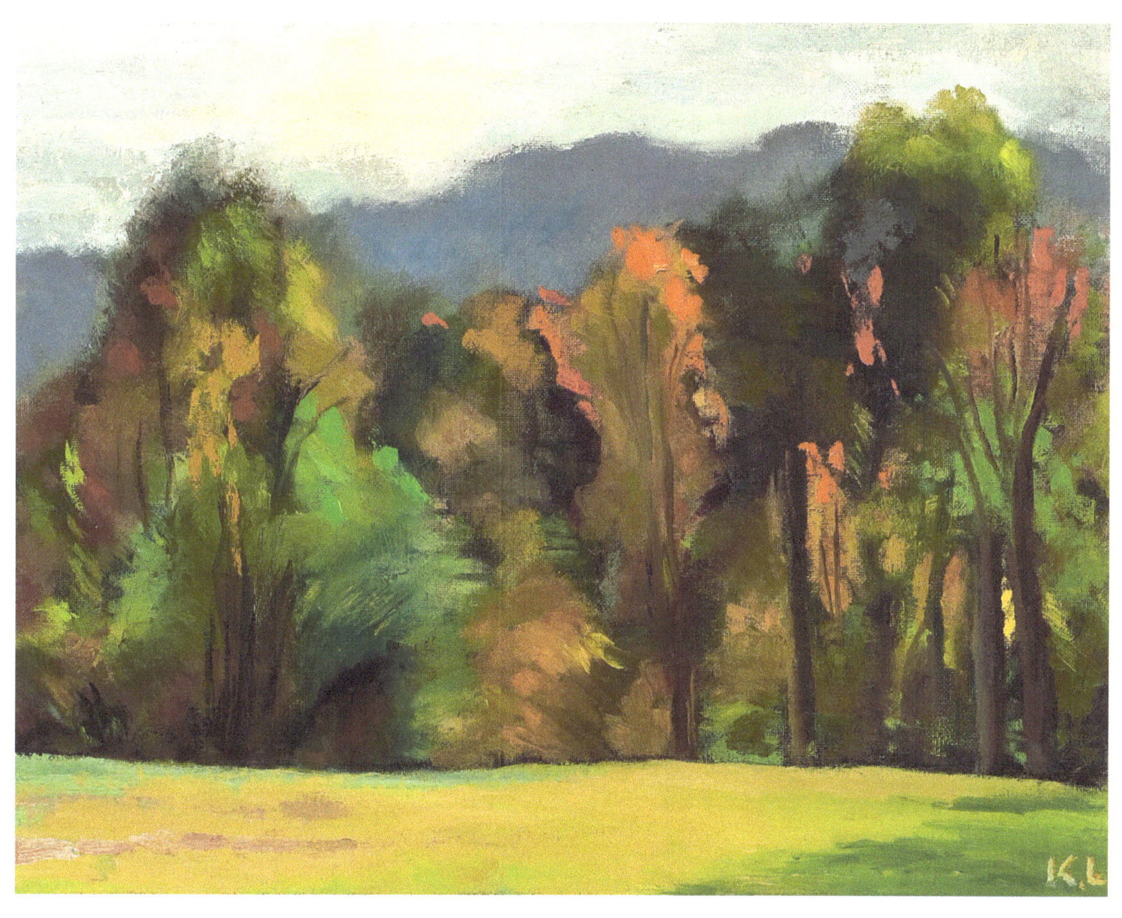

Autumn in New York by Kay Levine

MARGARITA

    —en honor a Kay Levine, *Margarita*

¿Cuántas cosas pueden condensar belleza?

¿Acaso solo unas bellas y coloridas flores?

¿Acaso un bello cuadro inspirado en ellas?

¿Acaso solo ellas existiendo allí afuera en el campo mirando al cielo?

¿Acaso la artista frente a ellas, construyendo ese bello recuerdo?

¿Acaso su hermosa talento solamente perennizado?

Acaso la bella sonrisa de mi madre cuando las recibe y

    guarda en el jarrón más preciado y recordado!

¡Acaso mi sonrisa cuando esas bellas flores esconden por detrás tres pequeñas y

    sonrientes caras!

MARGARITA

    —after Kay Levine, *Margarita*

How many things can condense beauty?

Just some beautiful and colorful flowers?

Perhaps a beautiful painting inspired by them?

Is it just them existing out there in the field looking at the sky?

Perhaps the artist in front of them, building that beautiful memory?

Perhaps her beautiful talent only perpetuated?

Perhaps the beautiful smile of my mother when she receives them and

    keeps them in the most precious and remembered vase!

Perhaps my smile when those beautiful flowers hide behind three small and smiling

    faces!

—Paola Vergara

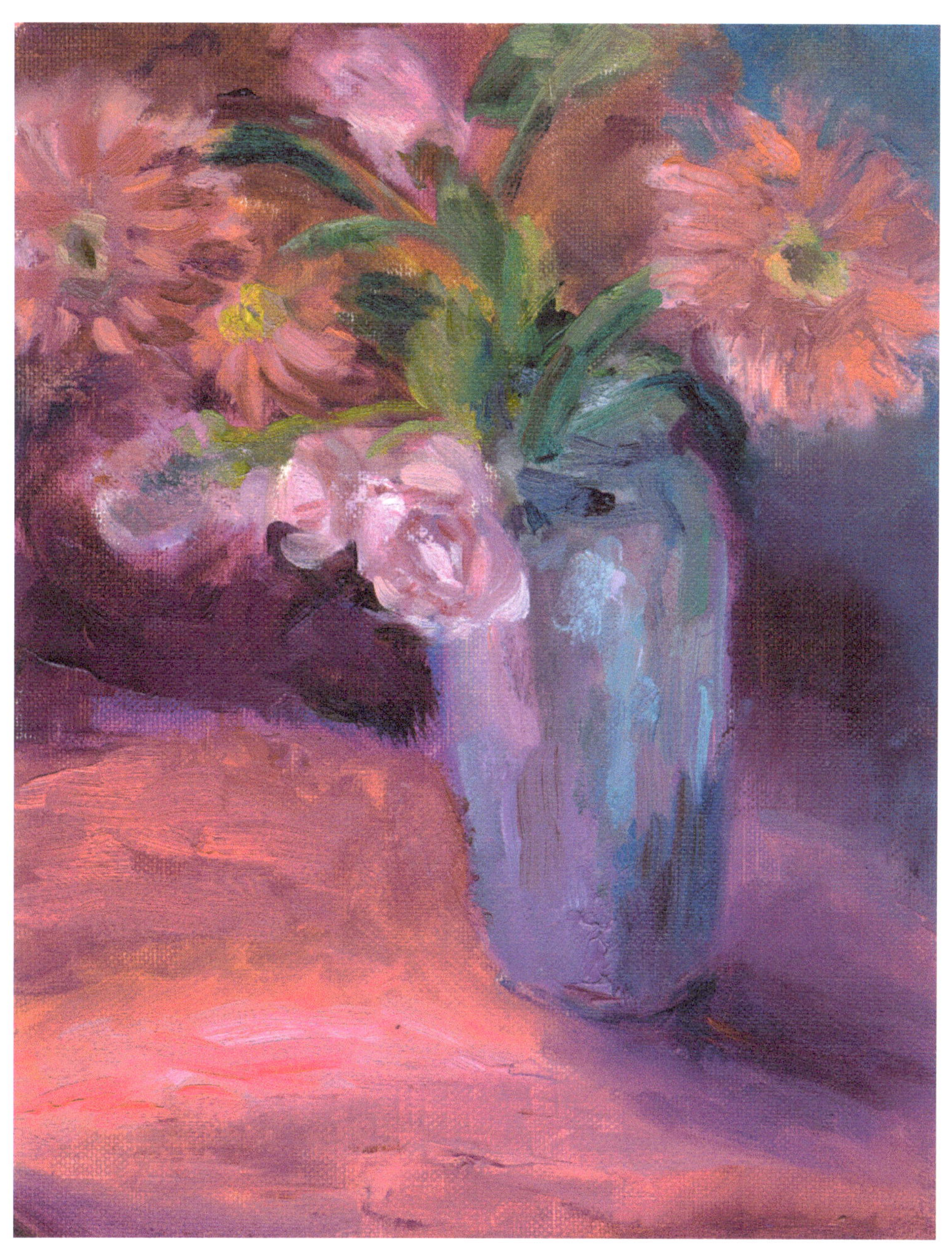

Margarita by Kay Levine

VERDE

    —after Kay Levine, *Fuscia and Green*

Two branches intersect in a glass,
then lean into their separate flourish

of blossom. Like family. Cut stems.
Separate destinies. An off-center base.

Some petals falling off, but most of them
lifting out into full expression, extending

from the baseline, that shared point
of overlap.

—Jennifer Dorner

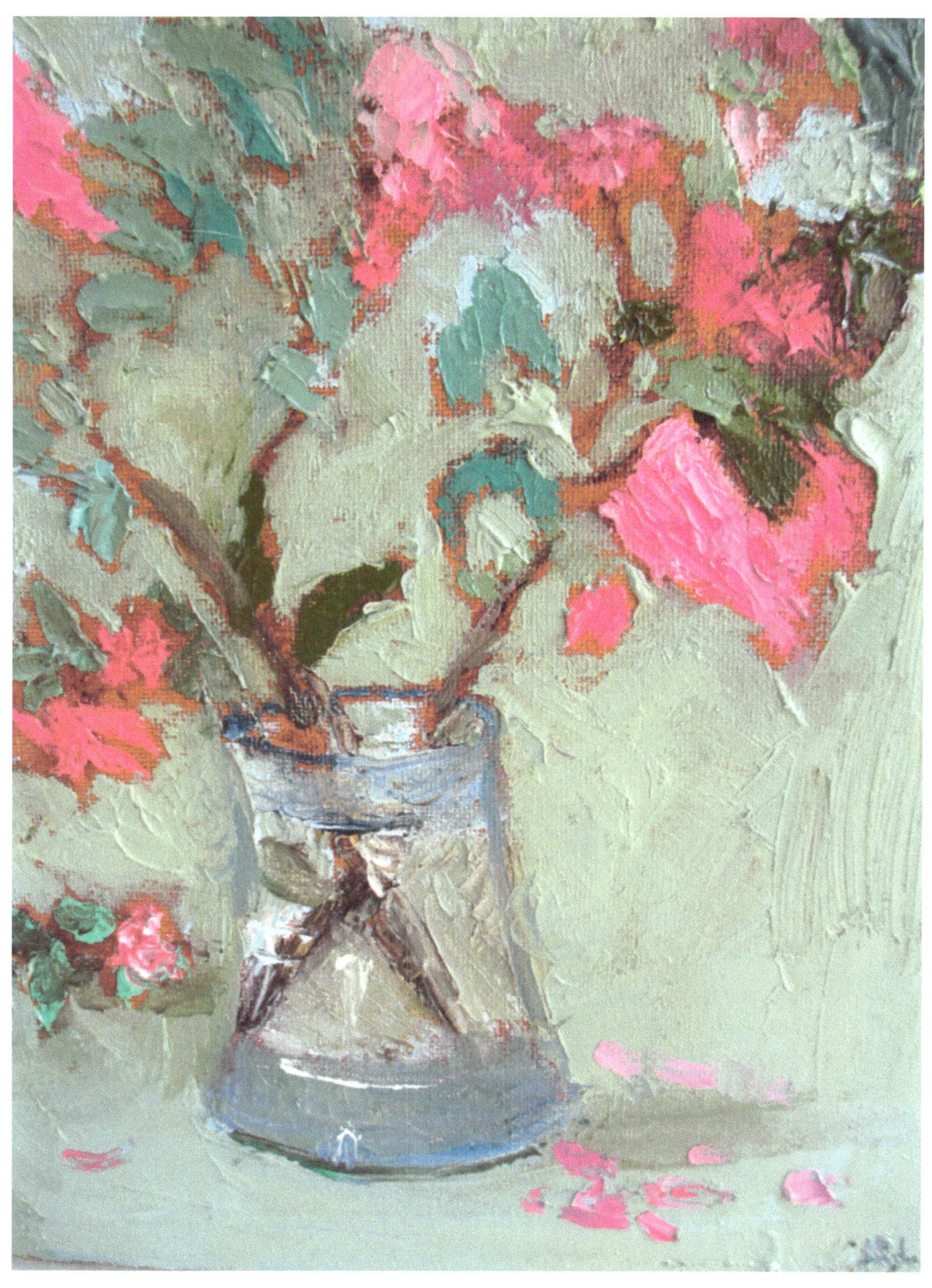

Fuscia and Green by Kay Levine

WOODSTOCK, NEW YORK

—after Kay Levine, *Woodstock, New York*

From behind a riot of indigo, gold, blue,
and magenta brush strokes that cover
that low hill, a grey dirt path curves into

the foreground. I lean closer and closer
to canvas until I stand in the picture, gritty
dirt under toes, grey pebbles dig into soles.

My soul aches to see behind that multi-hued
hill. I move along path's turquoise edge deeper
into purple dark. Colors drip on my clothes.

I wonder what I will discover in that place
the artist imagined but could not paint.
What dream of life might I create?

I turn right, vanish from sight.

—Peter M. Gordon

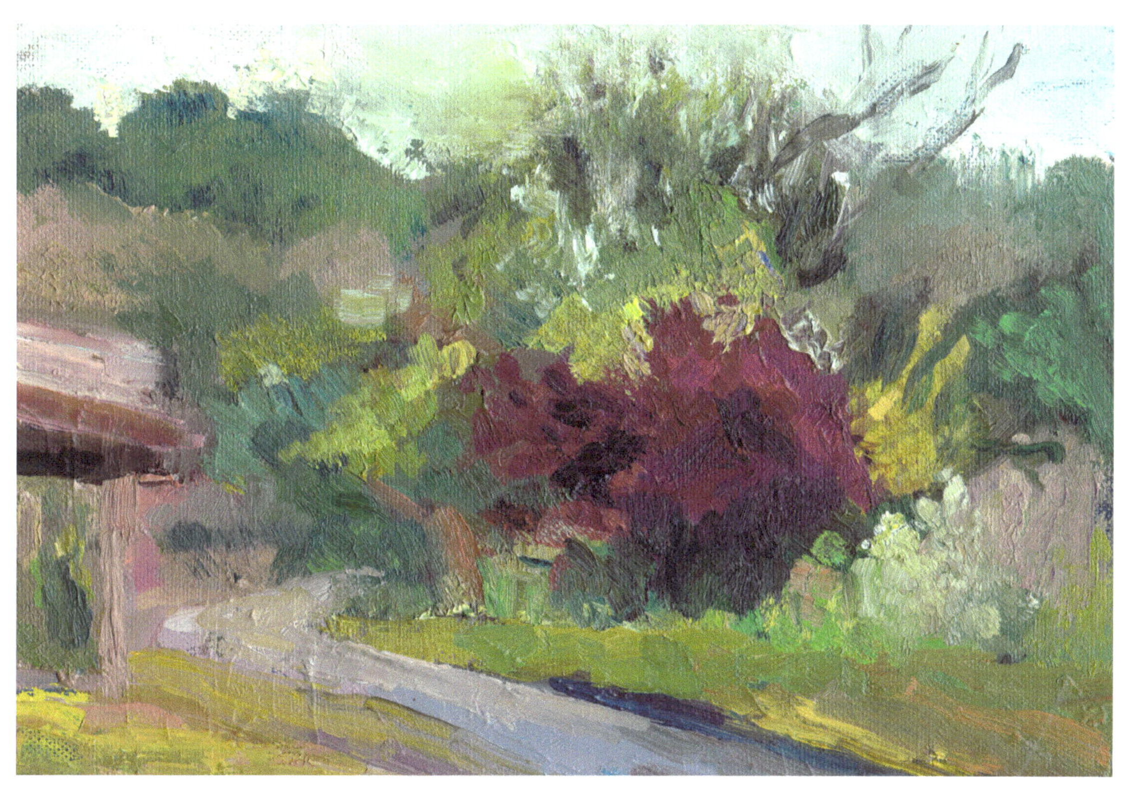

Woodstock, New York by Kay Levine

STILL LIFE FOREVER

—after Kay Levine, *Still Life Beside the Window*

Amber wine bottle attracts viewer with brush fulls of
golden yellow luster, melting down its sexy shoulder
through a stomach punch from a squatty, blue vase
pregnant with flowers—violet Lilacs or pink Dahlias.
Colors of weight give objects their place—brown, brushy black,
a river of shadow, for a life of stillness. White confetti tossed
all over the place assuring daylight. Forever. Potato,
two fruits, back to the amber bottle, viewer imagines
attempting exit through that glassy blue window into
the prettiest backyard in the neighborhood. Viewer will
never know for sure because this life is still. Realizing
her live thirst for just one, small glass of chardonnay.

—Norma Edythe Heyser

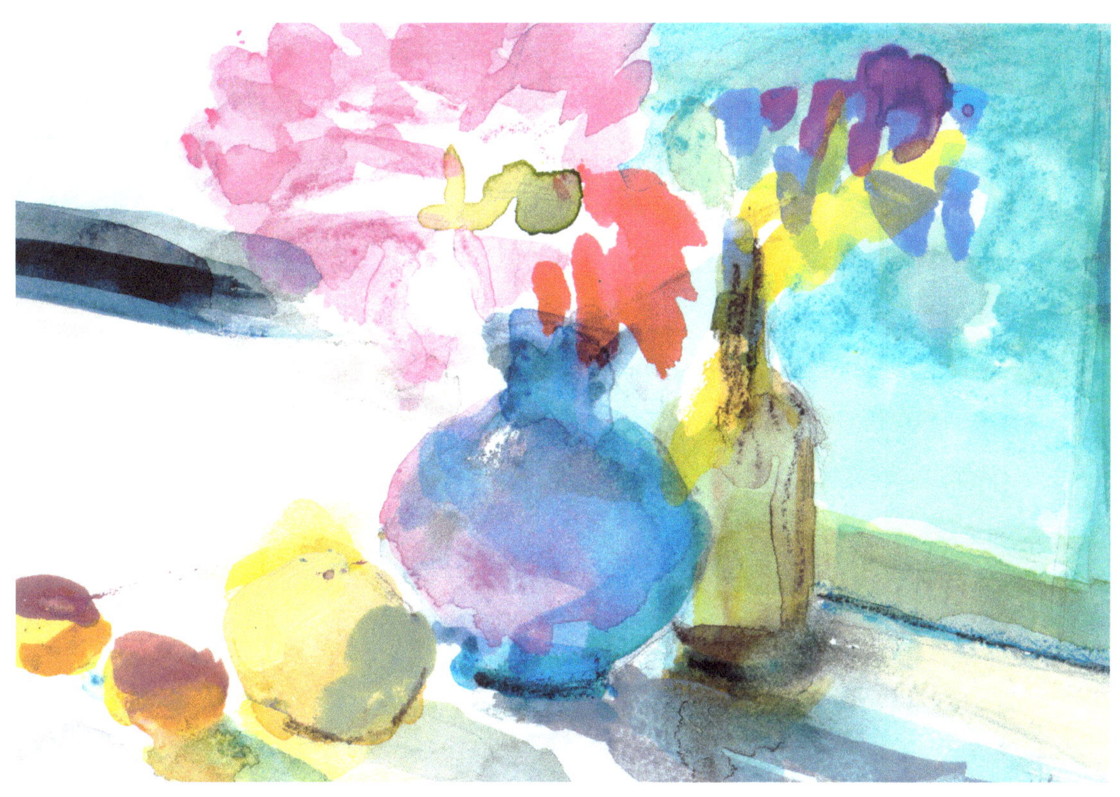

Still Life Beside the Window by Kay Levine

HEARTS OF FLOWER

   —after Kay Levine, *Solitude*

She is nine. She twists toward the wall
where an image of her heart, a pansy heart
flares violet like the ones circling
the white birch in the front yard—
a heart that yearns for her mother's heart,
a magnolia, those creamy white flowers,
ones her mother gilds and winds
through the bannister at Christmas time.
In that Plank-time flash she sees her mother
dying. Her hair, not ivory like the magnolias,
but white, white as clouds billowing in gray
skies, the color of her sad-soaked eyes.
Now her heart shrinks when she sees
purple-blue pansies and clenches
when she touches the smooth cream of a magnolia.

—Pattie Palmer-Baker

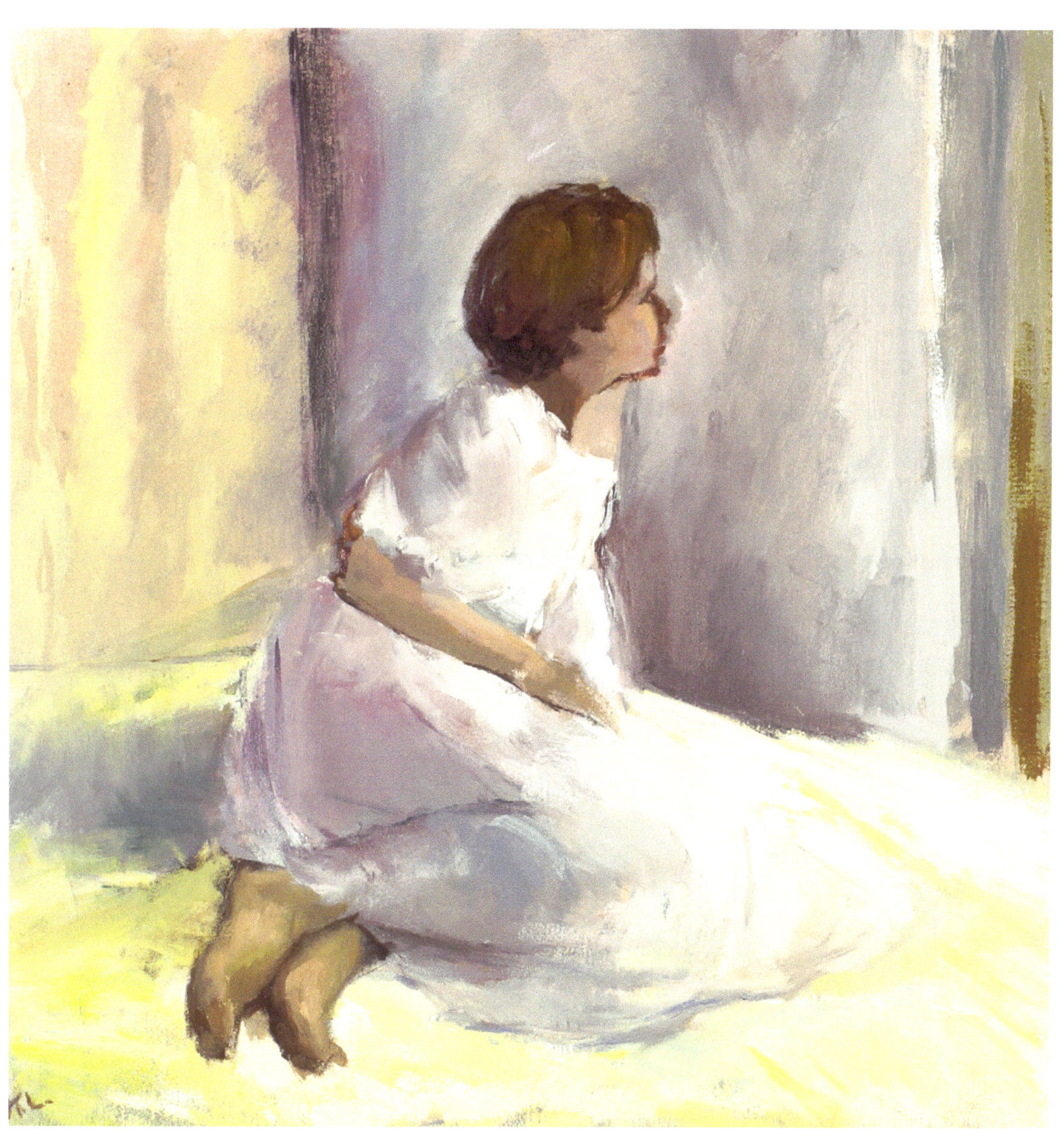

Solitude by Kay Levine

CALM BEFORE THE STORM

—after Kay Levine, *Calm Before the Storm*

In this calm, howling wind's hushed hues wait.

Laughing marshmallow clouds with blazing peaks

Cardstock blue—robin's egg blue—peek between.

Anticipation alters our landscape;

Pallet knife snicker-flies between colors.

Sepia water's reflection will fade,

A blush of words flies from unheard branches

Meanings from brushes cry like shredded leaves;

Distant sky, black bottomed boats and Greek fire.

But not now, not yet, vows your vicious wind.

—Marc Janssen

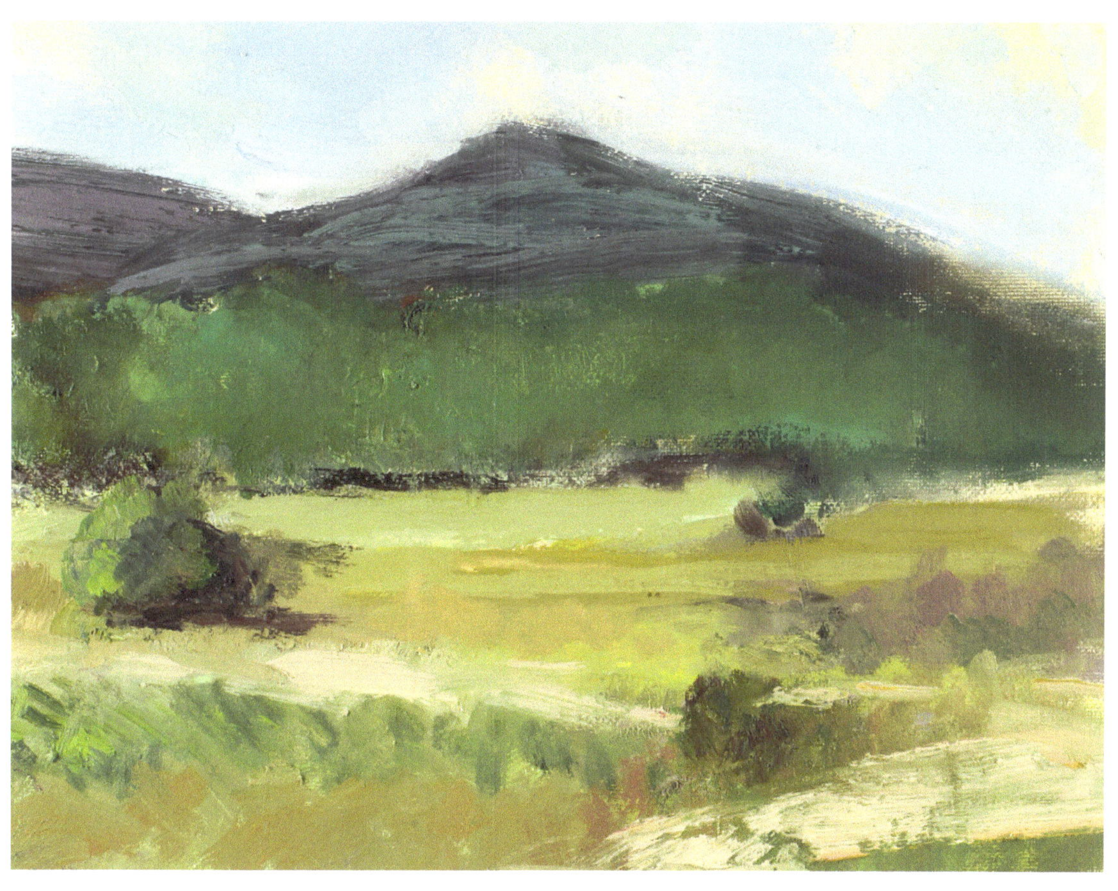

Calm Before the Storm by Kay Levine

—after Kay Levine, Two Trees

You, golden goddess, descend
from gray granite mountains
on words of wind, beckon

the last warmth of autumn.
Arrowhead leaves swirl in dance
amid shamanic dreams, layers

of amber, bronze, clay, evergreen
spirals, sandstone afternoons.
You welcome the voices

of children who emerge
as poets and wade
into oceans of streams.

—Francis Opila

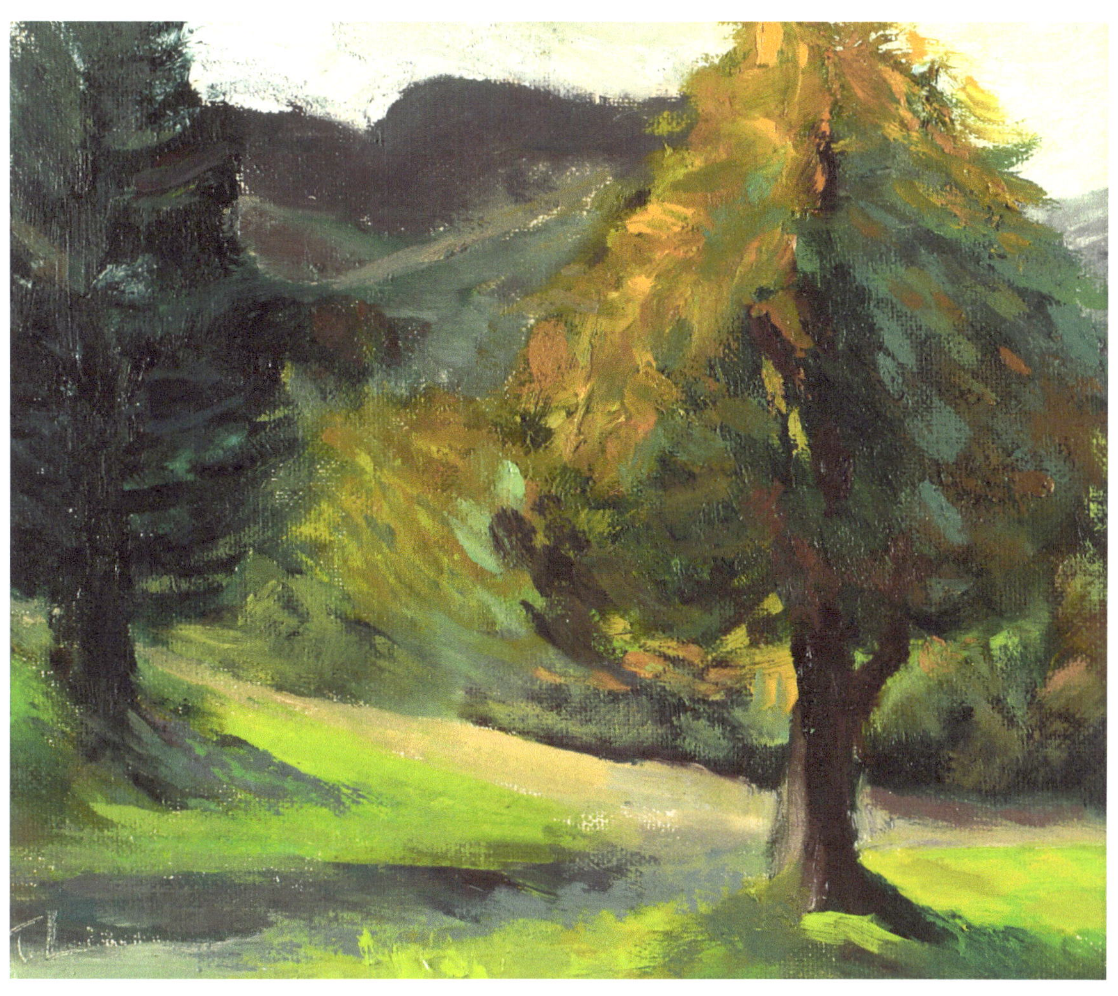

Two Trees by Kay Levine

DEAR KAY

—after Kay Levine, *Thank You for Every Gift*

Your card arrived while I
was upstairs in
the museum to study
Prussian blue, zinc white,
vermillion, chrome yellow
and see how the pigment
of a new palette opens
like a calyx. Your work
converses with both angel
and color merchant. I stared
to see what was under.
Indigo seed, chartreuse
seed, ghost seed sleep
in the earth. A root. And above
nested in shades of lavender,
fruit and tangle reach upward.
You're insistent: an ember
is behind each work, like a heart
behind the breastbone,
how there is only lush vibrancy
until we have none. A wasp
could land any moment amid
the abundance where the white
prairie baptisia,
the sunflower reach to the light.

—John C. Morrison

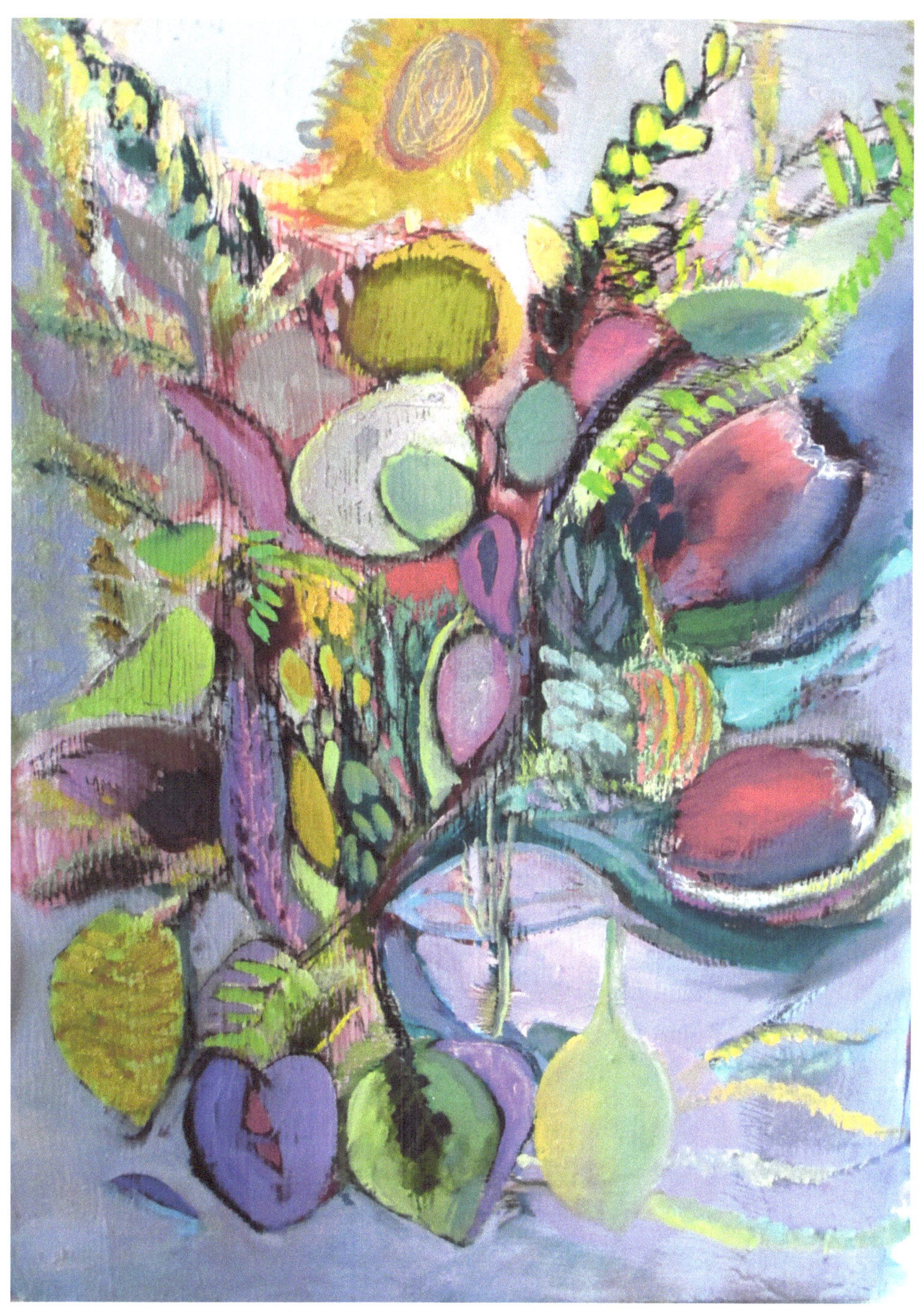

Thank You for Every Gift by Kay Levine

—after Kay Levine, *Windy Autumn Day*

When wind whirls leaves from the trees,
I raise both arms up into the sky,
to fly off with those leaves
over the blown grass,
fast, fast, faster,
until I'm gone
into the last
long song
of fall.
Goodbye. That's all. But maybe, maybe,
do you hear how I'm calling for you?
Maybe you could come too.

—Penelope Scambly Schott

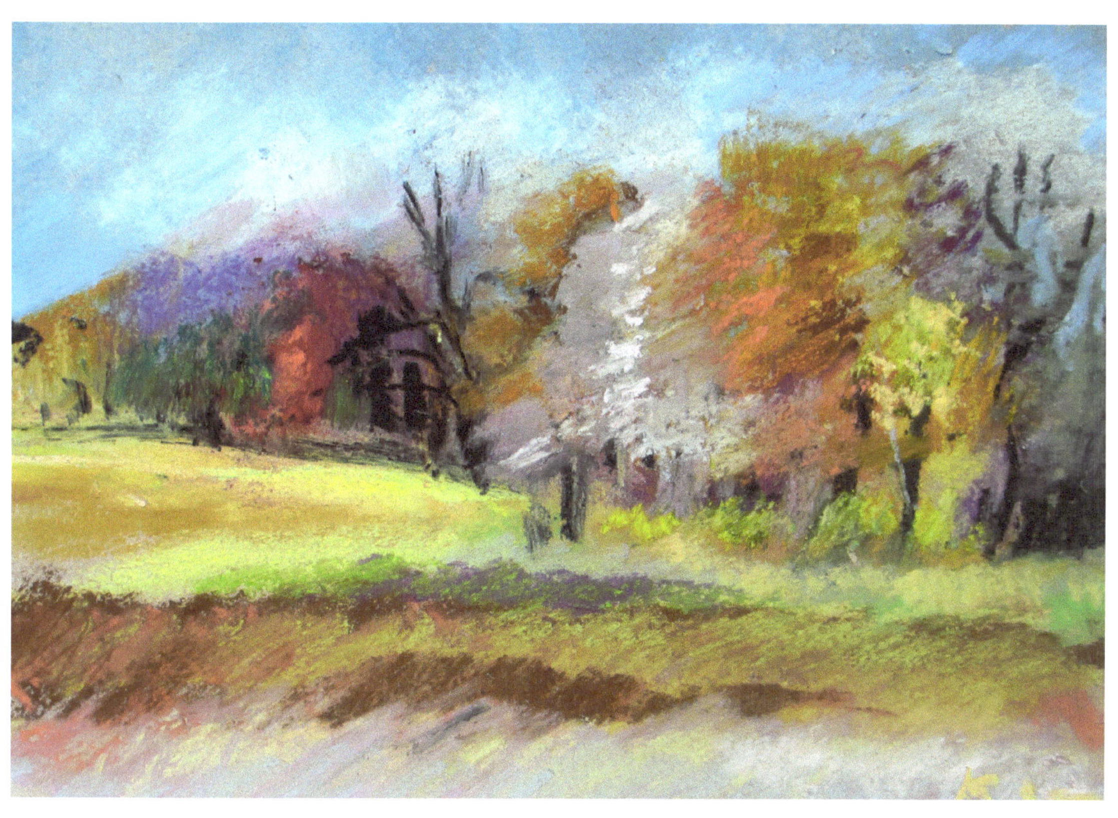

Windy Autumn Day by Kay Levine

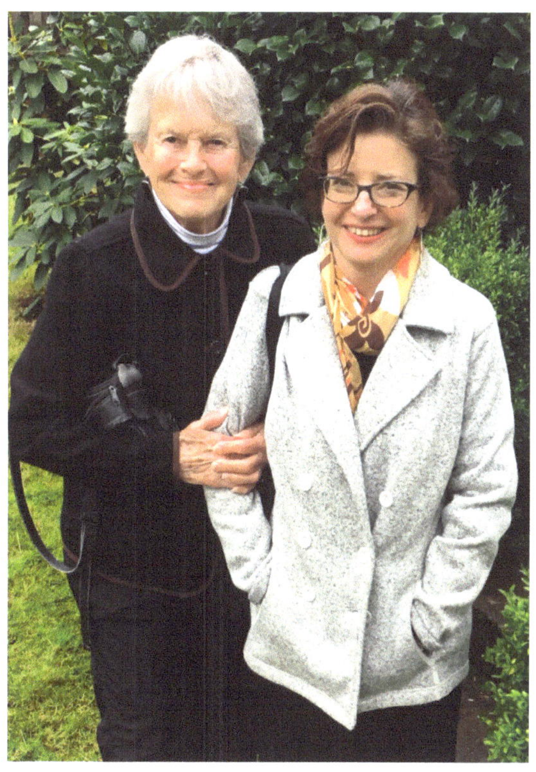

My mother and I inspired each other: me with my poetry and her with her art. She understood the hard work and joy of creating and always encouraged me to write.

For this project, I asked twenty-seven extraordinary poets to write poems in response to my mother's paintings. I was pleased and honored that they graciously and passionately responded with beautiful ekphrastic poems. This book is a gift and a celebration. My mother lives on through these paintings.

—Sherri Levine, Kay Levine's Daughter

No dark sunglasses, no hood over my head,
no scissors, shopping bag slung over my shoulder,

I slide behind bushes, pricked by brambles,
yank and snap, rip and tear.

No worry or rush,
or hush from the birds.

Squirrels, too busy collecting nuts,
don't stop on the lawn to judge.

Dandelion seeds fill the air like dust.
A silent sneeze, a cough caught in my throat,

I crawl under towering weeds
and hedges, wedge myself

between rocks and prickly thorns.
I do not feel the scraping of my knees

or the bee sting, burn of the sun
on my cheeks, heat on my hatless head.

Stealing flowers from the neighbors
I could only think of you in your hospice bed,

your weary head,
waiting for me to appear.

—Sherri Levine

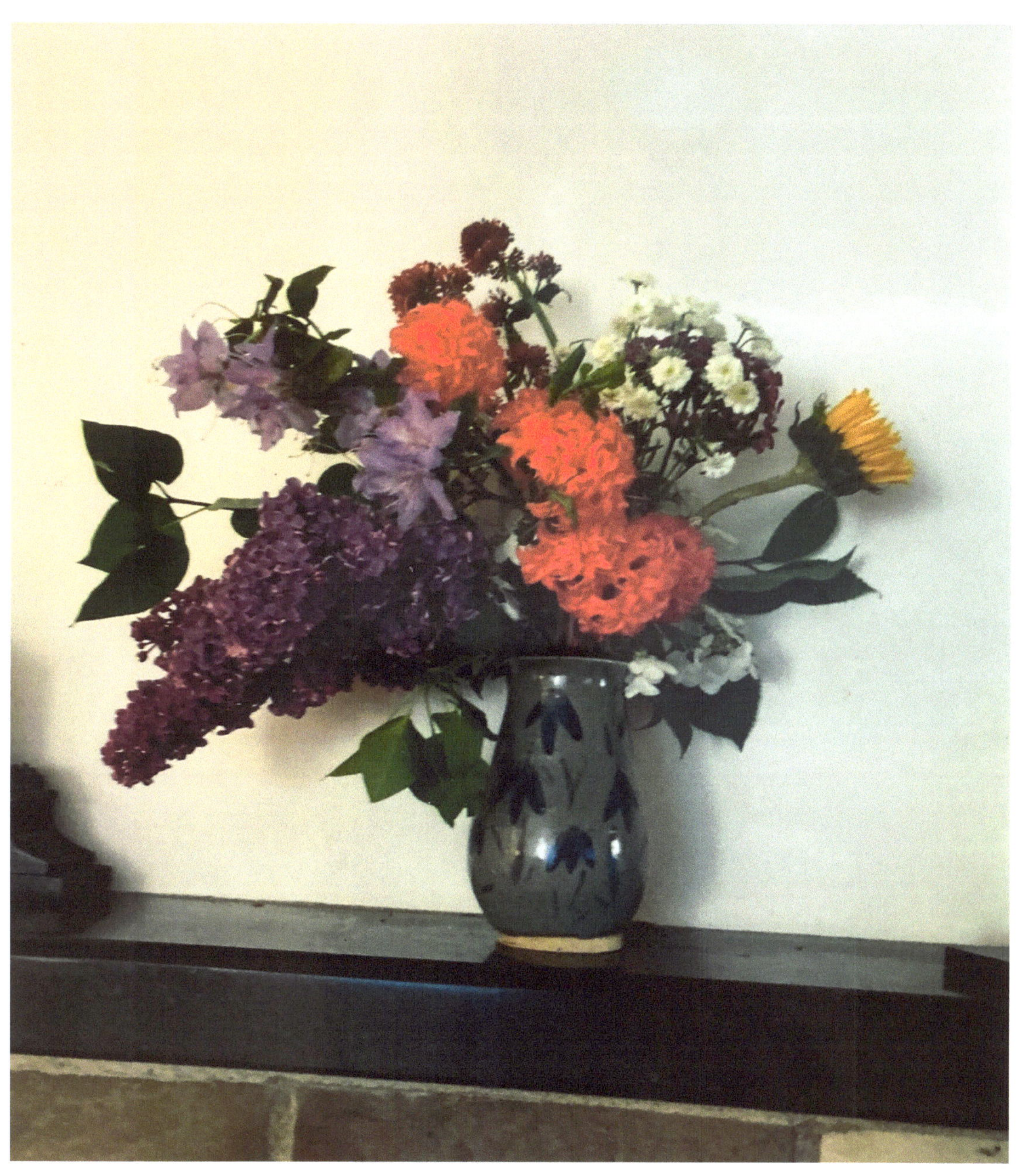

Thank you Neighbors, photo by Sherri Levine

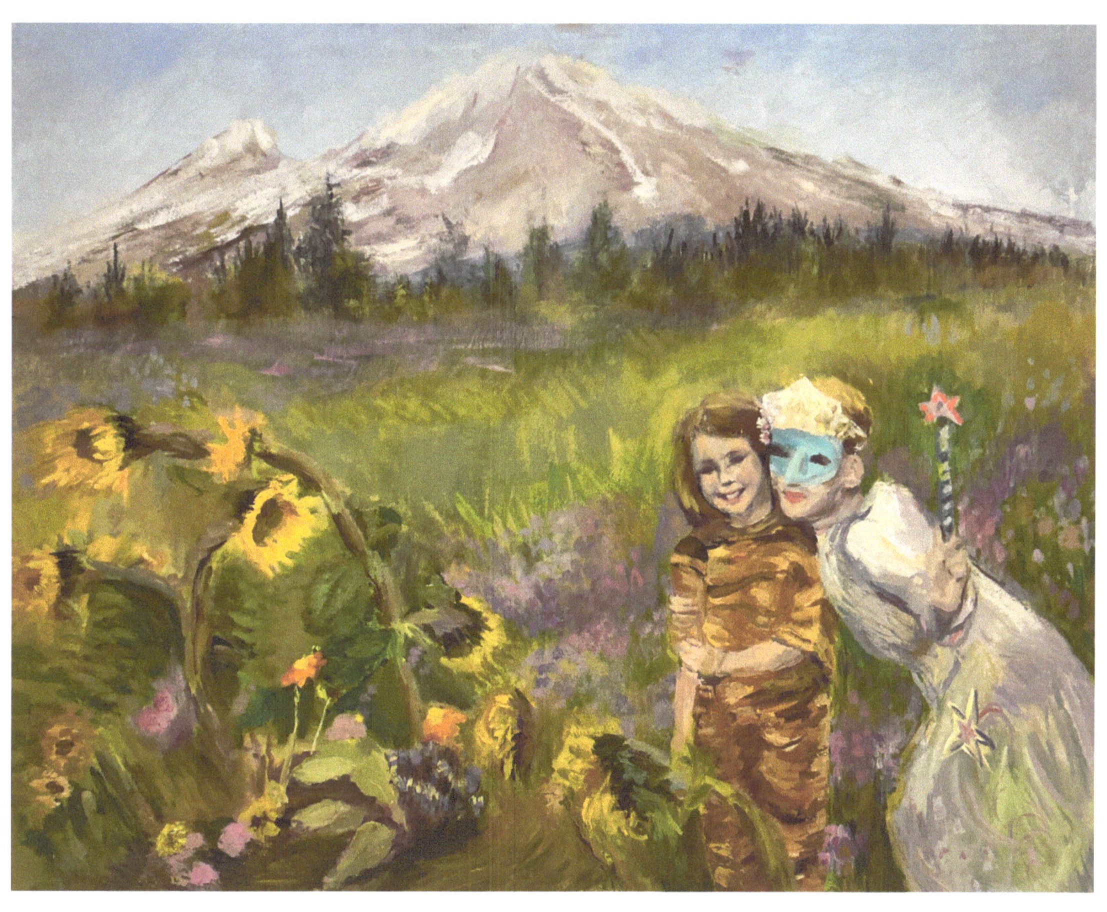

Sherri and her sister, Ann, costumed children in front of Mount Rainier, Painting by Kay Levine

IN GRATITUDE

to the poets who graciously and generously wrote
these ekphrastic poems

to the supportive and loving poetry community

to Ann Farley for her close attention to detail
in proofreading this manuscript

to Dale Champlin, my editor, publisher, and soul sister

to Kay Levine, my mother, whose paintings inspired the poets
and continue to inspire me

CONTRIBUTORS

Frances Payne Adler is the author of five books, *Raising The Tents*, *Making of a Matriot*, and three collaborative poetry-photography books and exhibitions. A portion of her current collaboration, *Dare I Call You Cousin*, tells about the Israeli-Palestinian conflict. She also co-edited *Fire and Ink: An Anthology of Social Action Writing*. Adler is Professor Emerita and founder of the Creative Writing & Social Action Program at California State University Monterey Bay.

Sebastián Arias is from Buenos Aires, Argentina now living in Pleasanton, California with his wife and two sons. He works as a freelance director, project advisor, and QC specialist of LatAm Spanish dubbing for different studios.

Shawn Aveningo-Sanders is the author of *What She Was Wearing*, revealing her #metoo secret—from survival to empowerment. Her work has appeared in *Calyx*, *Amsterdam Quarterly*, *American Journal of Poetry*, *Timberline Review*, and *VoiceCatcher*. A Pushcart nominee, Best of the Net nominee, co-founder of The Poetry Box press, and *The Poeming Pigeon*, Shawn shares the creative life with her husband.

Pattie Palmer-Baker lives in Portland, Oregon with her beloved husband and her quirky, elderly dachshund who writes odes to treats. Over the years of exhibiting her artwork—a combination of paste paper collages with her poetry in calligraphic form— she was delighted that many people, despite what they may believe, do like poetry; in fact, many liked the poems better than the visual art.

Dale Champlin, an Oregon poet with an MFA in fine art, has poems in *The Opiate*, *Timberline Review*, *Pif*, *CatheXis*, *Willawaw*, *Triggerfish Critical Review*, and elsewhere. She is the editor of */ pãn | dé | mïk /2020: An Anthology of Pandemic Poems*. Dale has published three books of poetry, *The Barbie Diaries*, *Callie Comes of Age* (Cirque Press 2021), and *Isadora*. Two poetry collections, *Leda* and *Andromina, A Stranger in America*, are forthcoming. *Medusa* is her most recent collection.

Nancy Christopherson's poems have appeared in *Aji Magazine*, *Amethyst Review*, *Cirque*, *Free State Review*, *Hawaii Pacific Review*, *Helen Literary Magazine*, *Hole In The Head Review*, *Kosmos Quarterly Spring Gallery of Poets*, *Molecule Tiny Lit*, *Verseweavers*, *Voice-Catcher*, and *Willawaw Journal*, among others. Author of *The Leaf* (2015), Nancy resides in Eastern Oregon.

Matthew Dickman is the author of *Husbandry*, *Wonderland*, *Mayakovsky's Revolver*, and *All-American Poem*. His honors include a Guggenheim Fellowship and the Sarton Award for Poetry from the American Academy of Arts and Sciences. Matthew has published widely. His debut collection, *All American Poem* (2008), was chosen by Tony Hoagland for the American Poetry Review's Honickman First Book Prize and also won the 2009 Oregon Book Award for Poetry. He lives in Portland, Oregon.

Jennifer Dorner's poetry has appeared in *Chicago Quarterly Review*, *Cirque*, *Cloudbank*, *New Ohio Review*, *San Pedro River Review*, *Sugar House Review*, *Tar River Poetry*, *The Inflectionist Review*, *The Timberline Review*, and other journals. In 2019, her poems placed 1st in Willamette Writers' Kay Snow Award for Poetry as well as 1st in two of Oregon Poetry Association's spring contests. She received her MFA from Pacific University in 2020.

Ann Farley, poet and caregiver, is happiest outdoors, preferably at the beach. Her poems have appeared in *Timberline Review*, *Third Wednesday*, *Gobshite Quarterly*, *Willawaw*, *Verseweavers*, *KOSMOS* and other journals. Her chapbook, *Tell Her Yes* (The Poetry Box), was published in April, 2022. She lives in Beaverton, Oregon.

Peter M. Gordon won the Thomas Burnett Swann Prize from the Gwendolyn Brooks Writers' Association of Florida. He's published over 100 poems in various magazines, and in two collections, *Two Car Garage* and *Let's Play Two: Poems About Baseball*. He's a founder and current President of Orlando Area Poets and hosts a monthly open mic for Florida State Poets Association. Peter teaches in Full Sail University's Film Production MFA program.

Leanne Grabel, a writer and illustrator in love with mixing genres, has produced numerous multi-media shows and illustrated works. Grabel is the 2020 recipient of the Bread & Roses Award for contributions to women's literature in the Pacific Northwest. Her graphic novel *Brontosaurus Illustrated* was released by The Opiate Books in July. Her chapbook of graphic prose poems, *My Husband's Eyebrows,* was released in 2022.

Nitza Hernández-López (aka Nitza Hernandez) is a bilingual Puerto Rican poet and visual artist living in Salem, Oregon. Her poetry has appeared in several printed and online anthologies such as */ pãn |dé | mïk /2020: An Anthology of Pandemic Poems*, *Antologías de Poesía Oregoniana*, *Terra Incognita* (Oregon Poets), *lalibreta.online*, *hojanegra.com*, *vozdevoces*, and *Pensive Journal*. She has won poetry awards from the Oregon Poetry Association and the Instituto de Cultura Oregoniana. Nitza also practices yoga and meditation.

Andrea Hollander's award-winning 5th full-length poetry collection is *Blue Mistaken for Sky* (Autumn House, 2018). Her many other honors include two Pushcart Prizes (poetry and literary nonfiction) and two poetry fellowships from the National Endowment for the Arts. After more than three decades in the Arkansas Ozarks, she moved in 2011 to Portland, Oregon, where she established The Ambassador Writing Seminars, now available through Zoom.

From the1950s, **Norma Edythe Heyser's** writing has evolved with her visual, conceptual and performance art commitments. In the 1990s she chose her writing teachers from Natalie Goldberg's Writing Practice, Tom Spanbauer's Dangerous Writing, Harold Johnson's Menucha Workshops, Steven Allred's basement table, and Joan Maier's Broadsides critique group. Her online blog is titled *So I See.*

Marc Janssen has been writing poems since around 1980. Some people would say that was a long time but not a dinosaur. Early decrepitude has not slowed him down much; his verse can be found scattered around the world in places like *Pinyon, Slant, Cirque, Off the Coast,* and *Poetry Salzburg.* His book *November Reconsidered* was published by Cirque Press in 2021. Janssen coordinates the Salem Poetry Project—a weekly reading, the occasionally occurring Salem Poetry Festival. Marc has been nominated for Oregon Poet Laureate.

Marilyn Johnston is an Oregon writer and filmmaker and a recipient of an Oregon Literary Arts Fellowship for Writers, as well as the winner of the Donna J. Stone National Literary Award for Poetry. The author of *Red Dust Rising* (The Habit of Rainy Nights Press, 2004) and a full collection, *Before Igniting* (Rippling Brook Press, 2020), she teaches creative writing in the Artists in the Schools program.

Sherri Levine is a poet living in Portland, Oregon. Her poetry has appeared in *Prarie Schooner, Poet Lore, Clackamas River Review, Jewish Literary Journal, Mizmor Anthology,* and other journals. She was awarded the Lois Cranston Poetry Memorial Prize by *Calyx* in 2019. She won First Prize (Poets Choice) and Second Prize in Oregon Poetry Association biannual contests. Her first full-length poetry collection, *Stealing Flowers from the Neighbors,* was recently published by Kelsay Press.

John C. Morrison has been a Portlander for some forty years. His poetry has appeared in numerous national journals such as *RHINO,* the *Cimarron Review, Poetry Northwest,* and the *Beloit Poetry Journal.* His most recent book, *Monkey Island,* was published by redbat books. He teaches poetry for the Attic Institute in Portland, Oregon, and is poetry co-editor for *Phantom Drift,* the fabulist journal of literature.

Susan Woods Morse grew up in California and moved to Maine in the early 1980s. She earned a Masters degree in Literacy Education at the University of Maine and taught English/Language Arts at the middle school level before retiring. Her poems have appeared in various journals including *Cream City Review*, *The Mom Egg*, *The Aurorean*, *Sixfold*, and *The Binnacle*. The effects of distance on relationships and relatives who have succumbed to Alzheimer's disease have influenced the poems in *In the Hush*, Susan's first chapbook.

Francis Opila has lived in the Pacific Northwest most of his adult life; he currently resides in Portland, Oregon. His work, recreation, and spirit have taken him into the woods, wetlands, mountains, and rivers. His poems have appeared or are forthcoming in *Parks and Points*, *Soul-Lit*, *Windfall*, and *Clackamas Literary Review*. He enjoys performing poetry, combining recitation, and playing Native American flute.

Paulann Petersen, Oregon Poet Laureate Emerita, has seven full-length books of poetry, most recently *One Small Sun*, from Salmon Poetry in Ireland. A Stegner Fellow at Stanford University, she received the 2006 Holbrook Award from Oregon Literary Arts. In 2013 she was Willamette Writers' Distinguished Northwest Writer. The Latvian composer Eriks Esenvalds chose a poem from her book *The Voluptuary* as the lyric for a choral composition that's now part of the repertoire of the Choir at Trinity College Cambridge.

Lois Rosen joyfully leads Salem, Oregon's Trillium Writers, the ICL Writing Group at Willamette University, and co-founded Peregrine Poets. Her poetry books are *Pigeons* (Traprock Books, 2004), *Nice and Loud* (Tebot Bach, 2015), and *Diving and Rising* (Finishing Line Press, 2021). She won Willamette Writers' 2016 Kay Snow Fiction First Prize and Crab Creek Review's 2021 Poetry Award. She's revising her novel-in-stories, *Junior Lifesaving*.

Emmett Wheatfall lives in Portland, Oregon. He is a published poet and lyrical recording artist. He has three books of poetry published by Fernwood Press: *As Clean as a Bone* (2018) and *Our Scarlet Blue Wounds* (2019), and his latest poetry book *With Extreme Prejudice: Lest We Forget* (2022). Emmett has recorded four albums and three singles of spoken poetry to music.

Lex Runciman's *Salt Moons: Poems* 1981–2016, was published by Salmon Poetry in 2017. *Unlooked For* is also from Salmon. An earlier title won the Oregon Book Award. Recent work has appeared widely, including in *The Gettysburg Review*, *Poetry Ireland*, *Hotel Amerika*, *Dime Show Review*, *Poetry East*, and *Valparaiso Poetry Review*. He lives in Portland, Oregon.

Willa Schneberg is a poet, essayist, sculptor, curator, and psychotherapist. She has six poetry collections including: *In The Margins of The World*, recipient of the Oregon Book Award, *Storytelling in Cambodia*, and *Rending the Garment*. Her work has appeared in anthologies and literary journals, including: *American Poetry Review*, *Salmagundi*, *Poet Lore*, *Bellevue Literary Review*, *Calyx*, and *The Journal of Psychohistory*. *The Naked Room* has just been released from Broadstone Books.

Penelope Scambly Schott is a past recipient of the Oregon Book Award for Poetry for *A is for Anne: Mistress Hutchinson Disturbs the Commonwealth*. She leads workshops in Dufur, Oregon, and she and her husband host the White Dog Poetry Salon in Portland. Recent books include *On Dufur Hill* and *Waving Flyswatters at Angels*.

John Sibley Williams is the author of four award-winning poetry collections, including *The Drowning House*, *Scale Model of a Country at Dawn*, *As One Fire Consumes Another*, and *Skin Memory*. A twenty-eight-time Pushcart nominee, John is the winner of numerous awards, including the Wabash Prize for Poetry, Philip Booth Award, and Laux/Millar Prize. He serves as editor of *The Inflectionist Review* and founder of the Caesura Poetry Workshop series.

Paola Vergara, originally from Peru, now lives in Arizona with her husband and three sons. She works as an engineer for a mining company. Paola loves art, reading, and spending time with her family.